GROW MOORE

THE SIX STEPS TO SUCCESS

IAN ELMORE-MOORE

GROW MOORE:
THE SIX STEPS TO SUCCESS

A Mindfulness and Leadership Development Guide for
Personal and Professional Growth

Printed in the United States of America
Noble Truth LLC, 2020
Noble Truth Project Inc.
2414 Herring Rd. #42705
Atlanta, GA 30311
www.nobletruthproject.com

TABLE OF CONTENTS

DEDICATION

This book is dedicated to 1) my Creator, 2) my Ancestors, 3) the entire Elmore-Moore family and 4) my friends. I thank you all for the encouragement and guidance you have given me over the years.

WARNING!!

THIS BOOK IS NOT TO BE READ ALONE INVITE A
FRIEND

PREFACE: YOU'VE ATTRACTED THIS

This preface serves as an introduction to The Noble Truth Project philosophy. Not to be confused with the Four Noble Truths of Buddhism, but the Universal Noble Truths that allow us to activate concrete change within our lives. Once you begin to read the following pages, your mind will unlock the Noble Truth outlined throughout each of the Six Steps to Success. These steps come with great responsibility, as you will learn that your successes and failures solely depend on you and you alone.

I am from Newark, New Jersey also known as Brick City; an urban metropolis located less than 10 miles from New York City. The city has been plagued with drugs, gang violence, and poverty since the infamous riots of 1967. During the early 1990's my city was declared "The Stolen Car Capital of the World." In the mid 1990's our public school system lost its accreditation to the state for a period of over two decades. Most notably in 2014, the U.S. Department of Justice released a report showing that the Newark Police Department had engaged in a pattern of unconstitutional conduct. To say my city has had a bad reputation is an understatement, but I survived. I avoided the medical examiner, the criminal justice system, and the welfare office with the support of my family, my faith, and most importantly, the Six Steps to Success.

I attended a private college-prep school starting in the seventh grade, graduated from the illustrious Morehouse College, and became a self-sufficient homeowner by the age of 23. I am a miracle, but the miracle would not mean anything to me if I did not give back to others.

I remember drafting the first proposal for The Noble Truth Project, Inc. It was during the winter of my senior year at Morehouse. I partnered with a fellow student and began to volunteer at the Fulton County Juvenile Court. After years of volunteering, we were given the opportunity to create a pilot program. We called it The Noble Truth Project, a weekly Saturday diversion program for adjudicated adolescents. We were referred ten youths, all of whom were identified as high-risk: gang members, drug dealers, and armed robbers; however we introduced them to the Six Steps to Success, and bolstered a 17% recidivism rate. We played a significant role in helping the young men we served transition into loving fathers, savvy entrepreneurs, and college graduates.

While running the mentoring program on the weekends, I taught middle school Social Studies during the week. I not only taught my students history, but the Noble Truth. Students loved to be in my class. I knew how to make my students successful despite competing challenges. I denounced the notion of "college for everyone" and taught my students the Six Steps to Success, however with the 2009 Atlanta Public School cheating scandal, the climate of public education in Georgia drastically shifted. I loved being a classroom teacher, but I became frustrated with the workload, curriculum changes, and teacher evaluations. I had the highest standardized test scores in the school, but one of the lowest teacher evaluation scores. This was a sign for me to move on. Within less than a year, I was appointed the Gang Prevention Coordinator for the Fulton County District Attorney's Office, the first gang prevention position within the state of Georgia. I have advocated for thousands of gang members and their families in the metro-Atlanta area by providing them with training, resources, and facilitating mediation.

Even though the program was successful, we struggled to be financially sustainable. The founding team moved on as we reached our organizational capacity. We had many successes, such as providing services to more than 500 youth, however also dealt with the harsh realities of losing some of our young people to prison and even death. Devastated by these events, I decided to relinquish my role as Program Director. Still, I hoped to spread the Noble Truth Project and the Six Steps to Success to a larger audience.

Several months later, I created The Noble Truth, LLC, a coaching and consulting company specializing in mindfulness and leadership development for personal and professional growth. By modifying our diversion program's curriculum, I have been able to provide assistance to a diverse group of people and corporations through the Six Steps to Success formula. If exposure to the Six Steps to Success can convert a gang member to a college graduate, it can also encourage schools, corporations, athletes, and individuals' seeking success in their personal and professional lives.

As an author, speaker, coach, and yoga instructor my goal is to shift minds and change lives. It is my intention to not only inform, but encourage individuals to look deeply within themselves, in hopes of curing such ills as trauma, poverty, self-doubt, fear, depression, and stress. Through the application of these six steps, one can go from a mental state of poverty and confusion into a mental state of bountiful wealth and purpose.

YOU'VE ATTRACTED THIS! Somehow, someway you've

attracted this book into your life. You've attracted the money to be able to purchase it or you've attracted the personal relationship in order for it to have been gifted to you. Regardless, you've attracted it. You've attracted everything around you. You've attracted your place of employment, your residence, your means of transportation, your friendships, and a host of other opportunities. When I first heard this NOBLE TRUTH, I denounced the claim. I could not phantom it. I attracted so many things I did not want in my life. I was a middle school Social Studies teacher and I hated my job. I did not hate my students, but I was dissatisfied with my salary and was overwhelmed by my workload. I woke up each and every day saying there has to be an easier way to make $50K. I was right; the way was through the Six Steps to Success.

The Six Steps to Success came to me through meditation, observation, and personal experience. I have used the six steps throughout my life and used them to help turn gangsters into graduates, employees into entrepreneurs, and homeless individuals into homeowners. We all hold unlimited potential within us. Success starts and ends in the mind. Once you are able to share your NOBLE TRUTH you will discover your PROJECT. We as human beings are resourced beyond measure as we are physical, mental, and spiritual beings. Before continuing on your journey to success it is important for you to understand 1) Who you are? and 2) Where you are? For these answers, I encourage you to join our community and receive our coaching services to learn more about your six intellectual faculties as well as the seven universal laws. We've attracted the good, the bad, and the ugly within our lives; however we can easily attract something new. WE ARE SPIRITUAL BEINGS, IN A PHYSICAL BODY, WITH INTELLECTUAL POWERS. Many people may know the Six Steps to Success, but few understand how to apply them. This book is written for those seeking tools of application. Read carefully and within these pages, you will discover the NOBLE TRUTH in each chapter. Be prepared to shift your mind, challenge old beliefs, and grow to your highest potential. Do not let this opportunity pass you by. Read carefully and attract the wisdom of success throughout each page. Namaste!

SET A GOAL: THE FIRST STEP TO SUCCESS

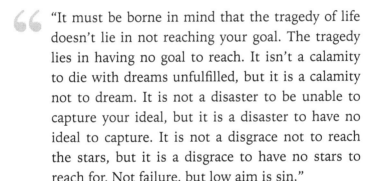

"It must be borne in mind that the tragedy of life doesn't lie in not reaching your goal. The tragedy lies in having no goal to reach. It isn't a calamity to die with dreams unfulfilled, but it is a calamity not to dream. It is not a disaster to be unable to capture your ideal, but it is a disaster to have no ideal to capture. It is not a disgrace not to reach the stars, but it is a disgrace to have no stars to reach for. Not failure, but low aim is sin."

— BENJAMIN ELIJAH MAYS

This is a mindfulness and leadership development guide for personal and professional growth. This book contains six steps for you to achieve success. Success is a unique word as it is simply used to mean an accomplishment of an aim or purpose. Success is not directly correlated to money; however it is connected to happiness. SUCCESS EQUALS PEACE OF MIND. Success comes to those who know what they want. Success is doing what you love to do and being able to live off it. If you are struggling to find your purpose, I recommend that you start to identify your talent. What do you naturally do well? What are you passionate about? What do you love? Talent mixed with passion will lead you to your purpose. Once you identify your purpose you can begin to translate it into your goal.

For instance, I am a talented speaker and passionate about mindfulness and leadership development. Both of these attributes ultimately have led me to my purpose, teaching. I have a desire to teach. I love to teach. This purpose has undergone constant improvements. Whatever you have in mind should be your starting place. I started as a public school teacher, then a co-Founder of a mentoring program, and became a Gang Prevention Coordinator. Ultimately, I came to the conclusion that the journey to fulfilling my purpose was by becoming a speaker and writer. Success begins with making a decision. Start with any goal that comes to mind and follow the six steps thoroughly. No matter what your goal is these six steps are designed to help you achieve your success. Remember, success is not solely about money, it is about obtaining peace of mind.

Talent + Passion = Purpose
Purpose + Goal = Success
Figure 1.1

How do you set a goal? To accomplish anything in this physical world we must first set a goal. If you work with youth in our public education system or in the criminal justice system, you may recognize that many of them do not know how to properly set a goal. Even college students and adults lack basic insight on goal setting. Everyone needs a goal to be successful. If a goal is not set correctly, it will never be achieved. HAVING AN INFINITE AMOUNT OF POTENTIAL IS MEANINGLESS IF IT IS NOT DIRECTED TOWARDS A DEFINITE GOAL. For several years, I struggled at goal setting because of my lack of definiteness. I was a jack of all trades, but a master of none. I launched The Noble Truth, LLC and experienced early success, however, I lacked definiteness.

During the first six months of launching my business, I had branded clothing for sale, yoga classes, motivational videos, inspirational quotes, and consulting services. I did everything, but yet, I had no focus. I had no true message nor was I showing improvement. I lacked the ability to improve because I lacked definiteness. According to authors Gary Keller and Jay Papasan, I lacked my "ONE Thing." I taught yoga five days a week, but hardly had the capacity to practice on my own time. The juveniles I instructed through the Department of Juvenile Justice (DJJ) got tired of yoga because I did not introduce them to new postures. I was holding them back. Not only because of my own insecurities, but also because of my lack of definiteness. If my definiteness of purpose was to become a yoga instructor then I would've taken those extra classes to learn new postures to teach them. I would've shown signs of growth, but because I put my time into other aspects of my business, I struggled to make progress in this area.

One day, I made a decision to have definiteness. I chose to master my Six Steps to Success philosophy. Even though I do yoga, I became intentional about rebranding myself so that people saw me as a speaker of my philosophy rather than just a yogi. With this declaration of definiteness, I immediately began seeing results. Definiteness provided me clarity on my priorities. Definiteness changed my thoughts and thus my feelings. Ultimately, this declaration led to different actions and produces different results. Definiteness is a defining characteristic of both success and failure. Definiteness is to be free of all ambiguity, uncertainty, or obscurity. Learn how definiteness allowed a 17-year-old to become the greatest of all time.

HOW A 17-YEAR-OLD BECAME THE GREATEST OF ALL TIME

In 2002, at the age of 17, LeBron James showed amazing definiteness, which has allowed him to become arguably one of the greatest professional basketball players of all time. Little do people know that in high school, LeBron James was not just considered the best basketball player in the country but also one of the best football players. LeBron got scholarship offers from Notre Dame University, Ohio State University and the University of Michigan as he was an all-state wide receiver. James, who earned first-team All-Ohio Division IV honors for two years straight after catching 61 balls for 1,245 yards and 16 touchdowns. During his junior season, he decided to quit football before his final senior season. At the age of 17, he had made a definite decision. He focused solely on basketball. He was not going to be a "jack of all trades," but become a "master" of basketball. When LeBron James set a definite goal, his career began to skyrocket. In 2003, during his senior year playing high school basketball, Sports Illustrated declared him "The Chosen One" and he has certainly lived up to that name. He is a 15 time NBA All-Star, four time NBA MVP, and three time NBA Champion. LeBron James has played in the NBA for over 16 years and has a current net worth of over $450 million. He has opened up a charter school in his hometown, signed a lifetime billion dollar deal with Nike, and has his own multimedia company. When we are definite with our goals success is sure to follow.

Figure 1.2

Goal setting is a skill set that should not be done in isolation. To goal set effectively requires definiteness but also, like all things, mindfulness. As a classroom teacher, each lesson I crafted required a S.M.A.R.T. goal. Traditionally, S.M.A.R.T. is an acronym that stands for specific, measurable, aligned, realistic, and timed. Classroom instruction needed to be intentional. Every lesson needed to be based on an academic standard. I remember walking into my classroom every morning and writing on the white board SWBAT, an acronym meaning, "Students will be able to," and in a 50-minute time block students must walk out of my classroom being able to master an objective. As an educator, I spent hours in professional development learning how to craft effective lesson plans and none was more useful to me than S.M.A.R.T. goal workshops. Management experts such as Edwin Locke, George Doran and Peter Drucker all highlight the important relationship between conscious goals, intentions and task performance. These three leaders affirmed that "specific hard goals produce a higher level of output". The principal advantage of S.M.A.R.T. objectives are that they are easier to understand and to know, when they have been met. The S.M.A.R.T. formula was an essential quality in developing a lesson plan and I realized that I could also use the formula to create plans for my life. With a few modifications, I constructed my own acronym for a S.M.A.R.T. goal.

A goal must be definite and S.M.A.R.T. The only significant change to my S.M.A.R.T. objectives is the use of "Serving" instead of the general term of "Specific." With definiteness as an overarching theme for goal setting, there is already specificity to the objective. Serving is the most important aspect of any goal becoming successful. If definiteness is your "what" then serving is your "why." In any business, one must serve. SERVING IS ESSENTIAL TO SUCCESS. My saying is "If you serve a million people, you'll become a millionaire; if you serve a billion people, you'll become a billionaire." Everything on this planet contributes something to living beings. Take time to view nature, as trees give us oxygen, rain gives grass nutrients, and even clouds give us shade. A universal law is the law of cause and effect. In order to truly receive we must first start by giving.

WHEN IT PAYS TO SERVE

"It's always good to do something you love," said Apple founder, Steve Jobs at the 2001 unveiling of the iPod. Steve Jobs was dedicated to service. In countless movies, books, and memoirs, Jobs talked about how he wanted to make the personal computer, the portable music player, and the cell phone more user friendly. His goal was ultimately rooted in people and as a result he grossed an amazing profit. In 2007 the iPhone was released. Even though Steve Jobs died in 2011, his estimated net worth was well over $2 billion. In just 2011 alone, Apple sold 72 million iPhones, 32 million iPads, 17 million Macs, and 42.6 million iPods. By 2016, Apple CEO, Tim Cook announced over 1 billion iPhones had been sold worldwide and by 2018, he announced over 2.2 billion iPhones had been sold. Service is necessary for life. Businesses must provide your customers with a service. Advancing the lives of others must be the crux of any goal you set. Without this essential quality success will never be acquired. Definiteness is your what, while service is your why. All goals need a sufficient what and why in order to overcome the test of adversity. During Steve Jobs's life, he experienced several challenges but was able to overcome them because of his burning desire to serve others. If you truly want success remember it starts with service.

All goals need to be definite as well as 1) serving someone other than you and 2) must be measurable. Measurable meaning your goal must contain a number. How many or how much? Answering these questions helps provide your goal with definiteness. With no number attached to your goal, you will never know when it is achieved. All goals must be data driven. In other words, it must include facts and statistics. For the purposes of effectiveness your goal needs to be analyzed. For instance, if your goal is related to fitness, how many pounds do you plan to lose? If your goal is related to finances, how much money do you intend to earn? If your goal is to increase your 3-point shooting, what is the percentage of shots you desire to make? If your goal is to rekindle a relationship, how many conversations do you wish to have with this person? A number is a fundamental requirement in setting a goal.

THE BILLION DOLLAR AUTHOR

One of best authors in the world, J.K. Rowling, had a measurable goal for obtaining success. She knew her magic number was 7. During her ride from Manchester to Kings Cross, she began to brainstorm, plan, and write the legendary Harry Potter series. In her five years of preparation, she made a definite decision that the series would consist of seven books. After drafting her first synopsis she was turned down by a majority of the leading UK publishing companies. In 1995, J.K.Rowling was newly divorced, living in a one bedroom Edinburgh flat, and had a six-month old daughter to take care of but she never adjusted her dream of writing all seven Harry Potter books. She wrote a majority of her first book on the train and in several coffee shops. In 1997, JK Rowling released *Harry Potter and the Sorcerer's Stone*, which has sold over 120 million copies to date, making it onto the New Year Times Bestseller list. In 2007, J.K. Rowling completed her goal by releasing her seventh and final book *Harry Potter and The Deathly Hallows*. In this amazing ten year time span Harry Potter made J.K. Rowling the first billionaire author grossing $7.7 billion in book sales, $8.5 billion in movie box office sales, $7.3 billion in toy sales, and $2 billion in DVD sales. All goals with a measurable number or percentage are bound to lead you on a successful path.

When setting any goal it must be measurable (containing a number). A goal must be definite as well as 1) serving, 2) measurable, and 3) aligned to your values. Many of us select a goal that is financially motivated. During my time at Morehouse College, I can recall several of my peers who hated their majors. They had no interest in becoming a doctor, lawyer, or financial advisor; however they chose these majors based on their projected salary. You will attract more money with a goal that is aligned with your values. Working at the District Attorney's Office, I encountered several lawyers who tried to persuade me to go to law school. One of the first selling points was how lucrative it would be. This is true, but being a lawyer is not in harmony with who I want to be. My goal is aligned with teaching, because I love seeing the lightbulb go off when others' receive knowledge. When you are goal setting, ensure that your goal is aligned with who you are and who you wish to become.

THE MAN WHO TURNED DOWN $50 MILLION

I remember watching CNN one day when the headline read, "Comedian turns down $50 million." I stared at the screen to see if this was a joke, but I learned it was not. It was comedian Dave Chappelle. In 2005, Dave Chappelle rejected a $50 million contract to continue his hit TV show. Dave Chappelle reportedly took a trip to Africa and shortly after his return decided not to sign a new contract. Dave Chappelle was ridiculed in the media. He disappeared from the public eye for over a decade. Dave Chappelle knew the material he was being asked to create on his TV show was no longer aligned with his values. He enjoyed comedy but his TV show was not a complete reflection of himself. This realization led him to turn down $50 million; however in 2016 Netflix reportedly paid Dave Chappelle $60 million for a three-part comedy special. Doing what is in alignment with your values will always be the right move.

A goal must be definite as well as 1) serving, 2) measurable, 3) aligned, and 4) realistic. One of the most difficult elements in creating a SMART goal is making it "realistic." The reason why is because everything is possible. Nothing is impossible. Thus, "realism" lies in the eye of the beholder. In the pursuit of your goal, you must believe in you, even when all others abandon you. There should be not a single ounce of doubt when developing your goal. YOU MUST HAVE UNYIELDING FAITH THAT YOU CAN MANIFEST YOUR GOAL. I vividly remember one of my fraternity brothers writing the definition of faith on my living room wall. It served as a daily autosuggestion that all things are possible. He wrote Hebrews 11:1 where faith is described in the King James Holy Bible as "the substance of things hoped for, the evidence of things not seen". Your goal must be realistic to you.

A CAR THAT MADE IT TO SPACE

Elon Musk, founder of Tesla and SpaceX is a great example of someone who sets realistic goals. Using his creativity, imagination, and definiteness he created the Tesla Roadster, the first highway legal serial production all-electric car. The Tesla Roadster uses only battery cells and is the first all-electric car to travel more than 200 miles per charge. Before 2008, auto manufacturers heavily scrutinized and doubted the Tesla Roadster. It was deemed impossible to create a long running electric powered car. When the Tesla Roadster was initially released in 2008, the country underwent a devastating recession. This recession destroyed American car companies such as Ford, GM, and Chrysler. Elon Musk lost numerous amounts of investors but never lost sight of his goal. When Elon Musk announced the release of the "Signature One Hundred", the Roadsters sold out in less than three weeks. It is now hard to drive anywhere in the United States without seeing a Tesla Roadster. A multitude of parking lots now have parking spaces designed specifically for the battery powered car to be charged.

Elon Musk forever changed the auto industry creating a product that others thought was "crazy" and he thought was realistic. In 2019, Elon Musk continued to challenge the notion of realistic goals with the creation of his newest company, SpaceX. SpaceX is the first private company to send a human-rated spacecraft to space. Elon Musk's goal is to transport humans to space, including the planet Mars. Elon Musk certainly does not believe in the word impossible as everything is realistic to him. He understands the golden rule of realism which is that goals must be realistic only to the one setting them.

A goal must be definite as well as 1) serving, 2) measurable, 3) aligned, 4) realistic, and 5) timed. The last step in creating a SMART goal is to put a date on it. Working alongside one of the greatest elected officials in the state of Georgia, District Attorney Paul L. Howard, Jr. taught me the value of putting a date on it. Goals need deadlines in order to monitor progress. In meetings, he would always pose a question, "what is the completion date?" He would stress the importance of having a timeline, deadline, and date on anything noteworthy. Time frames are essential to goal setting. They create a sense of urgency to the goal setter. Without this notion of time, a goal would always linger and lead to procrastination, which is definitely one of the main killers of all goals. The importance of timelines is perfectly expressed when looking at my own love story.

HOW A PERMANENT TATOO ENSURED A PERMANENT DATE

I met my wife, DeMecca, on August 18, 2006, at a friend's birthday party and soon after we started dating. Even though we were only in high school, we certainly loved each other. We would go on dates to the movies, IHOP, and visit each others' homes every weekend. In 2009, that all changed as I left New Jersey to attend college in Atlanta, Georgia. While I was gone, DeMecca decided to get my name tattooed on her ring finger and declared we would get married on the same day we met August 18. Her parents thought she was crazy for getting this tattoo and honestly, so did I. It was my first relationship and once I settled into college I saw beautiful women at Clark Atlanta University and Spelman College. I thought less and less of marriage. When we were both in college we did not talk as often, eventually breaking up during the second semester of my freshman year. Despite our breakup we reconnected and DeMecca came to Morehouse College on her birthday to attend my graduation. She was still living in New Jersey and I decided to stay in Georgia, which made it unlikely that we would rekindle our relationship. After my graduation, I needed support as I began to balance having a full-time job as a teacher. With lesson planning, athletic coaching, and grading I barely had enough time to cook, let alone eat. My life was upside down and I invited DeMecca to spend Valentine's Day weekend with me. I knew I needed to find some balance and DeMecca needed a fresh start. In 2014, DeMecca flew to Atlanta, for the holiday weekend and never left. The weekend was amazing as we laughed, ate, and talked about our future. During this time, she revisited her goal and declared that we were going to get married on August 18, 2018. I laughed it off, but could tell she was serious, so we decided to take it day by day. She did not board her returning flight home and officially moved in with me. We had several fights, arguments, and rocky periods, however she maintained that we needed to be engaged by 2016 and married by 2018 or else she would no longer be in my life. She put a date on it, stating that she could not waste time with me if I was not serious. On December 26, 2016 I proposed. She said, "Yes," and we made our vision come true by setting our wedding date to August 18, 2018. We had one of the BEST weddings on what is now referred to as the most popular wedding date in history. Make sure your goal is timed. Knowing a time frame creates an important element of definite- ness needed for all goals to be actualized.

Setting a goal is the first step to success. Goals require definiteness and must be S.M.A.R.T. Nothing else will suffice. Goals must serve others. Goals must be measurable. Goals must be aligned. Goals must be realistic. Goals must be timed. Goals most importantly need to be written down. World renowned educator Doug Lemov affirmed the importance of not only writing your goal down but also, "once your objective is complete, Post It in a visible location in your room". As an educator, I would be remiss if I did not provide you with an example of a proper goal, please see Figure 1.3.

I, Ian Elmore-Moore, will have $100,000.00 in my possession by 1st of January 2022. I am grateful to give my time, energy, and resources to operating The Noble Truth, LLC, a consulting company specializing in mindfulness and leadership development.
Figure 1.3

Until you outline your goal, you are wasting your time. Before moving onto the next chapter, please take out time to set a goal. Use my example provided above for assistance. It is imperative that you follow these directions carefully. I can only teach you from the experience I used to gain success. SUCCESS STARTS AND ENDS IN THE MIND. Success only becomes available through the application of the entire six steps working together in harmony.

STEP ONE: SET A GOAL SUMMARY GUIDE:

YOUR GOAL MUST BE DEFINITE
YOUR GOAL MUST SERVE OTHERS
YOUR GOAL MUST CONTAIN A NUMBER
YOUR GOAL MUST MATCH YOUR MORAL VALUES
YOUR GOAL MUST BE REALISTIC TO YOU
YOUR GOAL MUST BE TIMED

2

OVERCOME FEAR: THE SECOND STEP TO SUCCESS

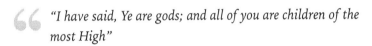 *"I have said, Ye are gods; and all of you are children of the most High"*

— PSALMS 82:6 KJV

The second step to success is to overcome fear. Many people have not achieved success because of their inability to overcome their fears. As long as I have been alive, I have not lived without the presence of fear however; I now have the tools to overcome them. Fear like many other things is simply a state of mind. One can truly overcome fear if you are tapped into the other five principles of this philosophy. Through sharing your NOBLE TRUTH you will overcome fear. Success requires courage. Courage like fear is a mindset. Spiritual teacher Don Miguel Ruiz affirmed, "we have a choice whether or not to believe the voices we hear within our own minds". You must develop a strong habit of choosing courage. No one's life is completely free of fear; they simply chose courage when fear is presented to them.

How do you overcome fear? My mentor once told me that

the word FEAR was an acronym that represents man's understanding of our creator's vengeance. He declared that people were fearful of FIRE, like the historic volcano eruption that destroyed the great city of Pompeii. He stated people were fearful of the EARTH, like the earthquake that devastated the city of Shaanxi. He explained people were fearful of AIR, like the beautiful island of Puerto Rico during Hurricane Maria. He proclaimed people were fearful of RAIN, like when the musical city of New Orleans experienced the flooding of the levees during Hurricane Katrina. Fire, Earth, Air, and Rain cause natural disasters in our environment, thus people became fearful of them. However, fear has evolved from this unique understanding.

None of my former students, people whom I coached or my mentees within the Department of Juvenile Justice, have ever indicated a natural disaster as one of their fears. All of the fears expressed to me were mental fears. Self-help guru Napoleon Hill explained "fears are nothing more than states of mind". Through meditation, observation, and personal experience I have outlined five major fears. I call these the Five Mental Fears. These Five Mental Fears are so dangerous that they can cause stress, sickness, and even death. Overcoming your fears is a vital component to you achieving success. I worked with countless colleagues who told me their goals and when I asked them what was in their way, 99.9% of the time it was one of these five mental fears.

Figure 2.1

Starting from the bottom and making your way up the list, what mental fears do you possess? If you have a fear of failure, you certainly will not become successful. A fear of doubt will prevent you from living your life to the fullest, scared to take any risks. The fear of criticism will paralyze you, making you unable to fully express yourself without stress. If you have a fear of being broke, you will limit the amount of money you will have in your possession. You may also limit your success if you have a fear of age. It is imperative that you thoroughly challenge these five mental fears. Take note of these true stories of how fear has limited the success of others.

THE FEAR THAT MADE IT TO THE BIG SCREEN

A student of mine was truly gifted. She could do her work fast and excelled in the classroom. However, when it came to her homework she never turned it in. She had amassed a perfect score on her participation, quizzes, and unit tests, but her homework score was holding her back. She was also an exceptional actress, performing in all the school plays and had a dream of one day being on the big screen. Her grade in my class and all of her other classes was 85%, losing 15% due to her missing homework. I pulled her aside after class one day and asked her if her home life was the reason why she could not complete her homework. I explained, "I would stay after school everyday for her to complete her homework in my classroom if necessary". She quickly refused. She stated "she did not want an A but preferred a B". Confused, I asked her "why"? She told me she "did not want to get all A's because she didn't want that pressure to get an A in everything". She was fearful of failure and as a result she was not truly living to her highest potential. I told her about making the Dean's List but she was satisfied with just the Honor Roll. By this point in my educational career, I did not persist and simply told her not to be fearful of failure. The fear of failure was limiting her achievement. Later that year, movie producer, Will Packer visited our school and awarded everyone on the Dean's List an opportunity to make a cameo in his upcoming film. The young lady was devastated. We took a field trip to the movies to see all of our students in the film and she began crying afterwards. When I asked her why she was crying she replied, "I'm going to get all A's from now on."

THE FEAR OF FAILURE IS A STATE OF MIND THAT WILL LIMIT YOUR SUCCESS. At the center of this fear is a lack of confidence. People believe they are not deserving of their awards. They feel they are unqualified and unworthy of achievement. When people suffer from the fear of failure, they believe they lack an essential quality that will breed success. They truly do not want to live up to their highest potential, ultimately leaving them to lead a life of mediocrity. Through the application of the Six Steps to Success one can overcome the fear of failure.

THE DEVASTATION OF SELF-DOUBT

One of my mentees enrolled in community college after

successfully passing his General Education Diploma (GED) exam. He was thrilled about his recent admission but became fearful of college. He knew he needed college to further his life but always saw himself as a high-school dropout. Even though he was admitted, he never attended a single class. When I confronted him on the issue of skipping class he told me "it was a waste of time and money." When I pressed further, he stated, "I am going to fail." I could never convince him to re-enroll and so he began to work at a nearby coffee shop. He served all the students at the community college that he would have attended. He saw them filled with fear and anxiety on their first day and witnessed them filled with joy and laughter on their graduation day. After working there for several years, he began to stop engaging with the customers as he became frustrated and depressed about his own life. He became a father of two and struggled financially to take care of them. He was in pain when I received a phone call from him several years later. He told me he had become the store manager, but still was not making ends meet. I suggested that he find another place of employment and he told me, "No," because he was fearful that he would not get the job due to his lack of education and inter– viewing skills. I told him his self-doubt had set him back and would continue to do so if he didn't change his mindset. When I went to visit him at the coffee shop, we sat and talked for a while and he expressed the same sentiments as he did on the phone. He shook his head and said he was comfortable. I gave him a hug and left the shop knowing that his self-doubt has caused him a lifetime of pain.

SELF-DOUBT IS A STATE OF MIND THAT BLOCKS SUCCESS. At the center of doubt is the lack of belief. People believe they will fail simply because they feel they are unqualified, unprepared, or unresourced. People fail because they stop believing in themselves. They believe they lack an essential quality that will breed success. The only two qualities that will breed success are faith and persistence. As long as you believe, you can achieve. Through the application of the Six Steps to Success one can overcome the fear of doubt.

THE COST TO POST

In 2013, I launched The Noble Truth Project, Inc., a mentoring program for adjudicated adolescents. However, very few people knew of the organization until its termination in 2019. No one knew about the great work we were doing each Saturday because of my fear of criticism. As an African American male, I was embarrassed to be an advocate for yoga and meditation and afraid of others' opinions. This fear of criticism was a disservice to not only the organization, but to the young men whom we served. Then, I could not see how documenting the program would have contributed greatly to the individuals who participated in it. I now know we live in an era of selling yourself or ultimately selling yourself short. Social media provides endless opportunities for growth, not criticism. Of course there are pros and cons to posting; however the pros certainly outweigh the cons. In 2019, I decided to relaunch The Noble Truth Project as a sole proprietorship, The Noble Truth, LLC. I knew I had to post in order to profit but I was scared of criticism from my friends, family, and colleagues. When I first released my weekly videos, people would share their opinions. I spent hours analyzing the comments of others. Everyone shared their opinions on how I could improve, however these critics had no videos of their own. Criticism can paralyze you from obtaining success. I learned to value the opinions of others, but never let these opinions overshadow my own beliefs. Since I began posting, I gained 1,000 followers within the first year and made over $10,000 in business trans– actions, specifically related to social media.

THE FEAR OF CRITICISM IS A STATE OF MIND THAT

WILL HINDER YOUR SUCCESS. In the pursuit of your success you will be criticized. It is important to remain positive and never allow the opinions of others stop you from moving forward. Criticism can be toxic if you allow it to become your reality. In Step Four: Tunnel Vision and Step Five: Gain Supporters I will talk more about how to properly disseminate the opinions of others. You must overcome criticism in order to be successful. Through the application of the Six Steps to Success, you can overcome the fear of criticism.

THE INVESTMENT THAT LEFT ME BROKE

One of my best friends was determined to be rich. He purchased several rental properties at a young age and did everything in his power to convince me to do the same. As a middle school teacher, money was clearly an issue for me. I had a few leftover dollars after each paycheck but was fearful to invest it. I put my money into my savings account in case of a rainy day. Meanwhile, my friend sold all of his properties and started to invest his money into government contracts. In order to secure the bid, it required him to take out a massive loan from the bank and begin immediate construction on a commercial property. The construction was delayed and he began to lose money quickly. He did not panic, but asked me again if I was interested in investing in the deal. This investment would help him get out of the hole and potentially make me more money. I refused again; scared to go broke as I thought it was a stupid investment. Even though I said, "No," he continued to invest, but all of his real estate commission money went directly to the project as he was forced to live back at home with his parents. With all of his loans, it was not long before he would have to file for bankruptcy. However, the project was finally completed. The government agency moved into his property and he immediately earned over $20,000 per month. This single deal made him a millionaire within 2 years. He moved out of his parent's home, purchased his own home, got married, and eventually quit his real estate agent job. He hit the jackpot and is now a real estate investor. Looking back on his achievement, I understood my fear of losing money, cost me money. My fear of going "broke" kept me broke and working as a middle school teacher.

THE FEAR OF BEING BROKE IS A STATE OF MIND THAT WILL PREVENT YOUR SUCCESS. It is kin to the fear of making money. The fear of being broke at one point in time stopped me from being an investor. Investors make money, but people believe that they are not worthy of having an abundance of money. The phrase "the rich get richer and the poor get poorer" is certainly a NOBLE TRUTH. Others make claims to justify their fear by stating "money is the root of all evil" or "life is not all about money" or even when being offered compensation saying, "I don't need your money" or "I'll do it for FREE." These are all the pitfalls of the fear of money. People do not acquire wealth because they do not pursue wealth. You must overcome a poverty mindset. I had a general fear of not making enough money and being scared to ask for a higher amount. I never asked an employer for a raise and in my early days never asked to be compensated for a speaking gig. The first time I asked for $1,000 for a speaking gig, I honestly thought it was too much. I thought my client would say, "No." I was amazed at the result and from that day on I have not charged any price less than that. Live in abundance and not in poverty. Through the application of the Six Steps to Success one can overcome the fear of being broke.

THE LIFELONG LEGAL ASSISTANT

As an employee of the District Attorney's office I get to meet some incredible people. One of them was an amazing legal assistant. He had been a legal assistant for nearly 20 years. Many of the lawyers, inexperienced and experienced would ask him for his advice during trial preparations. He was always seen throughout the office with a pep in his step. He drank nearly a gallon of water a day and was in tremendous physical and mental shape. One day I asked him if he was going to law school. He chuckled and abruptly said "No." He told me at one point in his life he truly had a desire to go. He had just begun working in the office and was gaining experience before he took the Law School Admission Test (LSAT). He said he had a child and that made him detour from his original goal. I asked him why he did not take the test today, as I assured him he would pass. He agreed, claiming he could beat many lawyers in court but proclaimed he was now too old. I did the math calculations in my head and told him he would be 47 by the time he finished law school and could practice law for another 25 years. He laughed but continued to state his time had passed. As we talked by the copier a veteran lawyer walked in. I asked him when he had become a lawyer and he stated, "I passed the bar only 10 years ago, I was 40." I looked at the legal assistant and he smiled back at me and said, "Ian, if I was your age, I would do it."

THE FEAR OF AGING IS A STATE OF MIND THAT WILL BLOCK YOUR SUCCESS. Age will come regardless; however, you should never let it prevent you from accomplishing your goal. It is important to remain positive and live a life that promotes positive mental health and physical fitness. Aging is a part of our transformative cycle of life. Age is not a sign to slow down or stop. Age is just a number. Many professional athletes such as Vince Carter, Venus Williams, and Tom Brady still compete despite their age. It is important for us to live to our highest potential. Focus on achieving your goal and do not focus on things that you cannot control. Through the application of the Six Steps to Success one can overcome the fear of age.

Overcoming fear is a challenge, but a necessary prerequisite for success. Fear is a state of mind, which can be changed. Pay close attention to the Five Mental Fears listed in this chapter and immediately begin to identify them. The sooner you identify them, the sooner you will be able to overcome them. For centuries, faith and fear have been deemed opposites. Faith is a positive response to something unknown, while fear is a negative response to something unknown.

Figure 2.2

Do you usually respond with faith or fear? Make a mental note of the figure above when you are faced with any and all decisions. Fear is our greatest enemy. SUCCESS STARTS AND ENDS IN THE MIND. Military General, Sun Tzu, once stated "if you know the enemy and know yourself, you need not fear the result of a hundred battles." Remember that fear will never lead one unto the path of success. Remember that fear will not bring about peace of mind. Do not move onto the next chapter without identifying and taking the necessary steps to overcome your fear(s). Through sharing your NOBLE TRUTH you will overcome fear. Remember to have faith, courage, and continue to adhere to the other five principles of this NOBLE TRUTH PROJECT philosophy, especially becoming more mindful.

STEP TWO: OVERCOMING FEAR SUMMARY GUIDE:

MASTER SHARING YOUR NOBLE TRUTH
MASTER YOUR FEAR OF AGE
MASTER YOUR FEAR OF BEING BROKE
MASTER YOUR FEAR OF CRITICISM
MASTER YOUR FEAR OF FAILURE
MASTER YOUR FEAR OF DOUBT

3

BE MINDFUL: THE THIRD STEP TO SUCCESS

 "The mind is its own place, and in itself can make a heav'n of hell, a hell of heav'n."

— JOHN MILTON

Be Mindful is a phrase many people use for a variety of reasons. As a yoga instructor, I often use the phrase to highlight the importance of breathing to my students. As a teacher, I used the phrase to make sure my students were paying attention to their sentence structure. Most recently, as a speaker and coach, I used the phrase to indicate the importance of being aware of your thoughts. "Be Mindful" is a keynote lecture I deliver, in which I ask my audience the question, "What is the most important body part, the heart or the brain?" See we only die if our heart stops working; however doctors proclaim us dead once our brain stops functioning. When the brain stops we are considered "brain dead" or in a "vegetable state." The term vegetable is used because we are still living like a plant but also immobile like a plant. No movement makes us unable to produce and unable to live to our highest potential. Keep in mind success equals peace of mind and it will only come through these six steps applied in unison.

How do you become mindful? In this context, being mindful relates to the knowledge of our thoughts. Being able to control your thoughts will lead you to success. British philosopher, James Allen proclaimed, "all that a man achieves and all that he fails to achieve is the direct result of his own thoughts." Our thoughts are energy. It's the "electricity" that makes the light-bulb function and emit light. The bulb in this case is our physical bodies or in scientific terms, "matter." Every scientist would agree that human beings and everything around us is a reflection of energy and matter. Thoughts come to us. Our ideas come to us. OUR THOUGHTS CONNECT US TO OUR UNIVERSE. Before moving on, I implore you to join our community and receive our coaching services to delve into a deeper understanding concerning the human mind and human brain. Be mindful that our brain consists of a brain stem (reptile), a limbic system (mammal), a neo-cortex (primate) and a prefrontal lobe (human). This is important because the understanding of our thoughts will ultimately lead us to our results. The mind, most importantly the subconscious mind, the powerhouse of our thoughts is the key attribute to us mastering mind- fulness. The subconscious mind differs from the conscious mind as it contains all of our beliefs that ultimately drive our behavior. WARNING: these results can either be positive or negative depending on the emotional state of our thoughts. We are only conscious while we are awake; however our subconscious mind is always operational. To make this complex reality simple, please see the figure below.

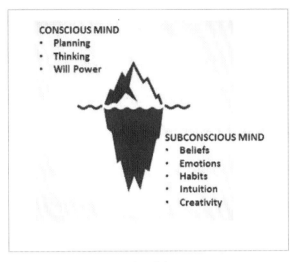

Figure 3.1

When our thoughts are emotionalized they become beliefs and these beliefs lead to our actions, and thus, our results. The only true way to become more mindful of our thoughts is to become aware of what we say and how we say it. THERE IS NO BETTER WAY TO EMOTIONALIZE YOUR THOUGHTS THEN FOR THEM TO BECOME WORDS. My mother would constantly say, "There is power in the tongue" and remind me that we can speak things into existence. As a practicing psychologist she knew how words lead to results. What you say leads to what you do. Your words and actions are the only representations of your thoughts. To become more mindful of your thoughts, you must master what you say. Spiritual Teacher, Don Miguel Ruiz stated, "through the word you can express your creative power. It is through the word that you manifest anything." To gain a level of success, you must continue to keep your words positive. Live in gratitude, live in forgiveness. Always be mindful of what you say as it is a representation of what you think, feel and will ultimately lead to what you do.

THE LITTLE ENGINE THAT COULD

As a youth, I remember the book, *The Little Engine That Could* as it played on the television or it was read to me as a bedtime story. The story begins with a shiny yellow train filled with toys on its way to a town on the other side of a mountain, but the engine shortly breaks down upon reaching the mountain. The train filled with toys flags down other engines to help them. The shiny passenger engine and big freight engine both refuse to help them and then, the rusty old engine is too tired and must rest. Finally, a little blue engine arrives at the mountain. Although she is simply a switch engine and has never been over the mountain, she agrees to help pull the train. In the end, she was able to successfully reach the top of the mountain before slowly heading down towards the town. The little blue engine always said, "I think I can," an important moniker for us all to live by. We can truly do all things just like this little blue engine. The key is we must think we can. We must hold positive beliefs about our own abilities. Many of us remember this catch phrase, "I think I can" but live our lives like the other trains saying, "I can't."

IT IS IMPERATIVE THAT WE MAKE SURE TO AVOID WORDS LIKE "TRY" AND "NOT." For instance, if someone says, "I will try to drive this car" their subconscious mind will hold on to the word "try." Try does not equate to success. Instead this person should declare, "I will drive this car." The word "not" holds the same weight on the subconscious mind. For instance, if someone says, "I'm not going to be sick," they are ultimately, affirming the negative as the subconscious mind will only react to the word "sick." Instead this individual should say, "I'm healthy." The idea behind "mean what you say and say what you mean" is critical to becoming successful.

THE POWER OF A SMILE

I'm not a Momma's boy; however I am my mother's only son. My mom is a veteran mental health professional, a licensed counselor, and longtime Supervisor of the PATH program. The PATH program provides case management services to individuals who are homeless or at imminent risk of becoming homeless and who have a serious and persistent mental illness. My mom would often fuss at me about anything. As a psychologist she would analyze everything I said or did. She would always say, "It's not what you say, but how you say it," which usually evolved into a 30 minute lecture. My mother would always question my body language, tone of voice, and facial expressions. She would always know when something was wrong with me. As a young man growing up in an urban environment you learn to show little to no emotion. Everyone raised in Newark, New Jersey seemed to have a "mean mug," a facial expression showing intense anger. I think the "mean mug" is a survival instinct, but my mom used to ask me what was wrong with my face. She would insist I smile. She would laugh and encourage me to laugh. I now know my mother understood smiling will change your mood instantly. As a professional psychologist she knew the mind could not tell the difference between what is real and what is imagined. SMILING WILL CHANGE YOUR EMOTIONAL STATE. For instance, when we experience a nightmare, we may wake up in a cold sweat. The nightmare is a dream; however, we cannot stop our bodies from automatically responding.

Psychologist, Dr. Joseph Murphy states, "your subconscious mind is the seat of your emotions. It is the creative mind. If you think good, good will follow; if you think evil, evil will follow...Once the subconscious mind accepts an idea, it begins to execute it." We all have a programmed operating system. Like cold sweats during a nightmare, a smile will produce dopamine, serotonin, oxytocin, and endorphins, all automatic responses that will begin to make you happy. ENERGY CONTROLS MATTER. So when we smile or have a physical response, the mind must be involved. The mind will act immediately upon thoughts that have been emotionalized. The best way to catch your emotions is to be mindful of the words that you speak. The word choice and tone of voice will matter as you begin the process of acquiring your desired goal.

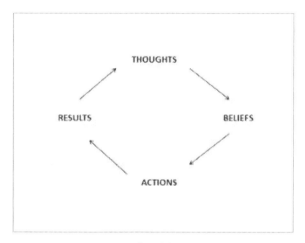

Figure 3.2

NO FLEX ZONE

There are so many examples of how people used "Step Three: Be Mindful" to become successful. Entertainers such as 50 Cent, Aretha Franklin and DJ Khaled understand the power of the tongue. In 2003, 50 Cent had a major break– through in the music industry. After years of mixtapes and battle raps, when his debut album *Get Rich or Die Tryin* was released he was a force to be reckoned with and 50 Cent affirmed his ultimate desire to "Get Rich" while overcoming the fear of death. Remember "trying" means your mind does not believe it will come true. Rapper 50 Cent was definite about getting rich and did not believe he would "die" as a result of his pursuit. The result of this album title was unwildering success. The album was #1 on the Top 200 US Billboard charts, went 6x platinum, and later became a movie. The film *Get Rich or Die Tryin* grossed $12,020,807 in its opening weekend and altogether, the film grossed $46,442,528 worldwide.

In 1967, Aretha Franklin demanded "Respect". The revised version of Otis Redding song became Aretha Franklin's signature song and was later hailed as a civil rights and feminist anthem. Franklin's version of "Respect" is a declaration from a strong, confident woman, who knows that she has everything her man wants. She never does him wrong, and demands his "respect". This declaration awarded Aretha Franklin with an astounding career. With 18 Grammy Awards, 20 No. 1 Billboard R&B singles, and over 75 million records sold. Aretha Franklin was without question "The Queen of Soul." She recorded for over 50 years and had 100 entries on the Billboard Hot R&B/Hip-Hop Songs chart, more than any other female artist. Her signature words became true, commanding respect in the male dominated music industry. Franklin was the first female inducted into the Rock & Roll Hall of Fame and Rolling Stone named her No. 1 on its list of the 100 Greatest Singers of All Time. Her long list of awards includes the Presidential Medal of Freedom, National Medal of Arts, Grammy Lifetime Achievement and a Hollywood Walk of Fame.

Similarly, producer, DJ Khaled, burst onto the scene in 2008 after years of working as a DJ for Fat Joe's rap label, Terror Squad. He grew to create "We the Best," his own record company. He says this affirmation in all of his songs and on his popular Snapchat and Instagram pages. In his book, DJ Khaled mentions, "You have to speak it into existence. You have to speak your success into existence...You need to own it with confidence and conviction. Say it to yourself first a thousand times." In 2010, DJ Khaled released his breakout hit song, "All I Do Is Win." The song went three times platinum and was even played at the 2013 White House Correspondents' Dinner. President Barack Obama was introduced to "Hail to the Chief," which quickly cut to a snippet of DJ Khaled's "All I Do is Win." Whether it is "All I Do is Win," "We the Best," "Bless Up", "Major Key Alert" or "Another One," DJ Khaled has mastered the art of being mindful of his words. These catch phrases have been extremely positive leading him to unlimited success.

If we believe we can't, there is no need for us to move forward because we will fail. Mentoring youth for years I have had countless conversations that would go like this, "Mr. Moore, I can't…" whether it was in the classroom, on the football field, or in an interview room. Once you commit to "can't" and the sounds "caa…" begin to roll off your tongue that thought has been crystallized into your subconscious mind and will affect your actions thereafter. I've always stopped anyone around me from using the words "can't" and "try," because I know we as human beings can do all things. If your thoughts are emotionalized they will become your beliefs and your beliefs will ultimately drive your behavior.

THE TEACHER THAT SHOUTED, "DEAD!"

One of my biggest pet peeves as a teacher was students' indecisiveness. I would call on a student's hand and they would start by saying,"Umm," "I don't know," "I can't," and "I'll try." I started to improve my student's public speaking and decision making skills through a game I called, "DEAD." I first started the game when I called on a student and they said, "try" and I quickly replied "DEAD!" The classroom was divided as some students began laughing, while others looked confused, and the young lady who initially spoke felt embarrassed. I silenced the room and said that everyone could shout out the word "DEAD" if anyone in class used the words "Um, I don't know, I can't, or I'll try." I proclaimed that if you say these words in a sentence I will no longer listen to you. The dialogue was "DEAD." Throughout the first quarter, "DEAD" was heard throughout my classroom. Students would scream it out throughout the day. During the second quarter, I began to hear it in the hallways. By the third quarter, I heard it in other teachers' rooms, and by the fourth quarter, I did not hear it at all. No one used these words anymore and as a result of this, we had one of the highest College and Career Ready Performance Index (CCPRI) scores in school history.

Words are powerful. This is why I say my affirmations daily. Through repetition I am reprogramming my mind with a positive mental attitude. "I AM SMART, I AM STRONG, I AM GREAT!" One thing that is great about being a human being is that we have the power to change. We can change everything. We can change our thoughts, behaviors, environment, appearance, and income all through obtaining mindfulness. The first element of mindfulness is mindfulness of the tongue. I have met countless individuals who tell me what they do not want for themselves and have yet to truly define what they do want. They have not been properly trained on how to correctly use their words to evoke change. Here is a quick story on how the words one young woman spoke changed her life forever.

A PHRASE THAT PASSED THE GED

A mentee of mine needed to pass her General Education Development Test (GED) in order to enroll in a cosmetology school. She failed her Math and Science exam over and over again. After months of studying, she began to become frustrated and wanted to quit. In this line of work, quitting meant reverting back to her former life of bank fraud. One day she called me and I could hear the depression in her voice as she asked me for help in passing these two exams. I told her everyday before studying, while studying, and after studying to go to her bathroom mirror and say, "My Mind is Divine." She laughed, saying that it would never work as we got off the phone. Later that year, I received another phone call from her asking me for a letter of recommendation into the cosmetology school program. Excited but confused, I asked her if she passed her GED test. She stated, "Yes, your suggestion worked." Unable to recall the suggestion, I asked her what she did differently. She stated when I brushed my teeth every morning and night I would look into the mirror and say, "My Mind is Divine." When I got the Math test a month later I kept saying the phrase as I took the test and I passed. I could not believe it, so I did it again for my Science test and I also passed. I will never forget what she said to me before we hung up, "Mr. Ian, thank you, sir. You were right, my Mind is Divine and that's the NOBLE TRUTH." Today this young lady is an entrepreneur operating her own all-inclusive salon in Atlanta. She services a multitude of high end clients, ranking in over a six-figure income, and is a loving mother of three.

Think before you speak. Think before you react. Thinking will stop unwanted results from occurring. The NOBLE TRUTH is taking a few moments out of your day to breathe. It will have a dramatic impact on your results. I remember sharing that statement the first time I conducted a yoga class. The yoga class was inside the Fulton County Juvenile Court. It was filled with young men between the ages of 12-17, who were all adjudicated for a full range of crimes. My mentoring program bolstered a 17% recidivism rate because we focused on shifting minds and changing lives. We understood changing their thoughts would lead to them changing their actions. How did I get young African American men involved in criminal activities to do yoga? I took it day by day. The first part was enabling them to notice the power of breathing.

Breathing slows down our minds, ensuring adequate time for our brains to receive oxygen. Breathe is the primary way in which we can clear our minds of unwanted beliefs. Buddhist Monk, Thich Nhat Hanh affirms, "our breath is like a bridge connecting our bodies and our minds." Breathing is also a key component of meditation. Meditation is a practice where one focuses their mind on a particular object in order to achieve a mentally clear and emotionally calm and stable state. Learn how my yoga practice helped others make better decisions.

HOW BLUNTS LED TO MINDFULNESS

I vividly remember my first time teaching yoga to youth within the Fulton County Juvenile Court. They were apprehensive, to say the least. They had never done yoga before and thought it was an activity solely for girls and White people. I expressed to them that I practiced it and explained that it would help them calm down. I began to speak about the practice of meditation. One of the young men began to hum and said he was a monk as the entire room burst into laughter. I was embarrassed, but I did not give up. I simply asked them a question, "how many of y'all smoke?" Their hands immediately shot up. I asked them to demonstrate how they smoked a blunt of Atlanta's finest weed. The group continued to laugh, but one young man stepped up and took a large inhale holding his breath for a moment before he exhaled. I asked him how he felt and he said that he felt the same. I instructed him to do it several more times. I again asked him how he felt and he replied, "better." He said, "it is almost as if I had the blunt for real, no cap." Everyone began laughing again, but I challenged them all to do it. After the first 15 minutes of laughter, the room fell silent as everyone was practicing a deep ratio breathing technique. I asked them how they felt and a majority of them said that they felt, "good." That day, we did not do a single yoga posture nor a meditation, but my first yoga class was deemed a success. I had gotten them to breathe. I had gotten them to be mindful.

Breathing is a way to calm down our minds. According to the National Science Foundation "our minds receive 60,000-80,000 thoughts per day". This is an overwhelming amount to any human being, especially our youth. They sometimes lack the ability to regulate their thoughts and end up acting upon all of them. This would lead to diagnoses such as ADD or ADHD. Even though these diagnoses are real, as a teacher I have seen countless youth wrongly diagnosed. They are then prescribed drugs that make them unresponsive. Instead of medication, I think they should've first been referred to a yoga class. Psychologist, Travis Bradberry and Jean Greaves declare "breathing right {is} one of the simplest yet most powerful techniques that you have at our disposal to manage your emotions." BEFORE REACTING TO A SITUATION, TAKE A MOMENT TO BREATHE. By regulating your breath you will calm down your mind, enabling you to make the best decisions instead of an impulsive one.

Being mindful about your thoughts is the silent key to success. Truly successful people have trained their mind to block out all negativity. The two ways to become more mindful of your thoughts is to 1) watch what you say and 2) breathe. The words that come out of your mouth have amazing powers. We do "speak things into existence." The power of the tongue can bring forth life or death. What we tend to say is what we tend to do. Every word you choose to use has been filtered through your mind. Keep in mind, it is not only what you say but also how you say it. Make sure to speak slowly or speak with your eyes closed to ensure that you are speaking words of success.

Breathing has changed my life. I cannot put it into context the benefits I have gained by adding meditation to my day. During meetings, speaking engagements, or yoga classes I always take a second to breathe. Buddhist Monk, Thich Nhat Hanh states, "every moment of our daily lives can be used to cultivate mind- fulness." While driving, washing dishes, or taking a shower, I breathe. Walking the dog, using the restroom, and eating dinner, I breathe. My asthma has greatly improved because of my ability to regulate my own breathing.

Being mindful is one of the Six Steps to Success. It is a fundamental principle to the NOBLE TRUTH. Our thoughts will lead to our actions. Success starts and ends in the mind. We must become mindful of what we say and how we say it. These emotionalized statements will lead to our successes or failures. Before we speak, we must think. By taking a moment to breathe we will give our brains adequate time to process our thoughts before they are expressed into words. Do not move on until you begin to become mindful of your thoughts, words and actions. Live in gratitude, live in forgiveness. BELIEFS DRIVE YOUR BEHAVIOR. If you don't like the results you are receiving you must change your thoughts. The way to master becoming more mindful is through practice and adhering to the other steps to success.

STEP THREE: BE MINDFUL SUMMARY GUIDE:

COMMIT TO SMILING
COMMIT TO BEING POSITIVE
COMMIT TO OBSERVING NATURE
COMMIT TO MEDITATING DAILY
COMMIT TO BEING PRESENT
COMMIT TO AVOID SAYING "CAN'T" & "TRY"

4

DEVELOP TUNNEL VISION: THE FOURTH STEP TO SUCCESS

 "You must be the change you wish to see in the world."

— MAHATMA GANDHI

Tunnel Vision is focusing on a single goal. In this context, Tunnel Vision, relates to utilizing audio and visual suggestions to create thoughts that ultimately will assist you in acquiring your desired goal. As human beings we cannot turn off what we see nor what we hear, however, we do have the power to control what we hear and what we see. As Buddhist Monk, Thich Nhat Hanh describes "without mindfulness in our daily lives, we feed our anger and despairs by looking or listening to things around us that are highly toxic". Tunnel vision requires us to have repetitive discipline to only see and hear material that specifically relates to us achieving our desired goal.

How do you develop tunnel vision? We all heard of the phrase, "monkey see, monkey do." It highlights the power of our minds. I remember watching movies such as *The Dark Knight*, *Drum – line*, *Stomp the Yard*, *ATL*, and *Enter the Dragon* and what a profound impact they had on my life. After watching *The*

Dark Knight and E*nter the Dragon*, I would pace around my room doing all sorts of karate moves. So much so, I once bruised my hand by punching my bedroom door. The films *Drumline, ATL*, and *Stomp the Yard* completely changed my life. I walked out of *Drumline* asking my mother to buy me a snare drum kit. After *ATL*, I went to the skating rink for the next year to perfect my moves. I loved the film *Stomp the Yard* so much that I decided to go to Morehouse College in Atlanta, Georgia and ended up pledging the into Omega Psi Phi Fraternity ultimately, competing in a multitude of step show performances. The fact that I knew I would walk out of a good movie and start to act as if I was a leading character in the film made me aware of the power of visual and auditory suggestion.

Branding is not just a marketing practice in which a company creates a name, logo or aesthetic that is easily identifiable. BRANDING IS ALSO A NEUROLOGICAL PRACTICE THAT IMPRINTS THOUGHTS INTO THE MIND. Billions of dollars are spent each year branding your brain. The popular show *Mad Men* was based on this practice. The show, *Mad Men* is set primarily in the 1960's at a fictional advertising agency on Madison Avenue in New York City. The show highlights the introduction of the television being a focal part of life and how the world of advertising is all about conditioning us to make a decision based on what we see and what we hear. Every successful company has an advertising division. Business mogul, Grant Cardone stated, "if people don't know who you are, then they cannot do business with you...You have to be known, thought about, considered, and hopefully, the first or dominating choice in your clients' minds in order to ever sell anything to anyone." Driving through Downtown Atlanta, I am reminded of the show *Mad Men* when I see billboards from some of the most famous companies, Home Depot, Coca Cola, and Delta Airlines. When I stop to get gas before heading home I see posters everywhere enticing me to walk inside the service station and make a purchase. There is enormous power in what we see and what we hear that drive us to action.

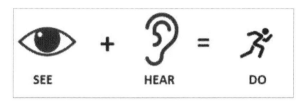

Figure 4.1

An important element of obtaining tunnel vision is to be auto–suggestive. If we know we can crystallize our thoughts into beliefs by our audio and visual senses we must create these suggestions everywhere. If you spend a day with me you would know I am all about the NOBLE TRUTH PROJECT and teaching others the Six Steps to Success. If you walk into my house today you will find me wearing a Noble Truth Project logo T-Shirt, a vision board in my office, and a multitude of awards on my wall. You couldn't be around me longer than two minutes without hearing a positive affirmation. Affirmations are positive statements that can help you overcome self-sabotaging and negative thoughts. For instance, one of my favorite affirmations comes from self-help psychologist, Emile Coue: "Everyday in every way I am getting better and better." My vision board is also a tool I use to help clarify, concentrate, and maintain focus on my goal.

I remember watching an episode of *Oprah's Master Class*, an interview with Steve Harvey talking about his goal for his daytime talk show. He sought to make his talk show one of the best on daytime television. His number was 1.7. This number represented the 1.7 million daily viewers he wished to have tuning in. He desired that number so much, he had it stitched on the inside cuff of all of his shirts. Steve expressed how he would be recording and take a moment to glance at his stitching. This glance immediately made him more energetic and grounded in his goal. He was obsessed. A stitch that made him rich was a useful auto suggestive technique. Steve Harvey knew he needed to visualize his goal in order for it to manifest.

THE SURGEON WHO SCORED A 520

Gabby was a Spelman senior who had a goal of becoming a plastic surgeon. Her goal had several short term goals within it. Besides passing organic chemistry, her biggest challenge in undergrad was to pass her Medical College Admission Test (MCAT). This exam would ultimately be a defining part in her acceptance and enrollment into the nation's top medical school. When it came down to choosing a measurable goal, no number was of more significance than the number 520. Gabby wanted a 520 on the MCAT exam, so much so, she began to apply the principle of Tunnel Vision within her life. Gabby had created an amazing vision board that she looked at as soon as she woke up and before she went to bed each night. Gabby posted 520 throughout her dorm room, cell phone wallpaper, and set her alarm to both 5:20am and 5:20pm. She studied with a definite purpose. If you asked her, "What was her favorite number?" she would easily respond with 520. The first time Gabby took the MCAT exam she scored an astonishing 522. She surpassed her 520 goal and was six points away from a perfect score. Gabby achieved her goal as she was admitted and enrolled into the nation's top medical school on a full scholarship. Gabby had achieved one of the highest MCAT scores in school history and went on to become a leading plastic surgeon in the metro Atlanta area. Gabby's tunnel vision and use of her vision board was a key component to her success. It provided her with a visual suggestion to entice her to continue to pursue her goal.

A vision board is any sort of board in which you display images that represent whatever you want to be, do, or have in your life. I completed my first vision board during my senior year of college. It was a class assignment after viewing the movie, *The Secret*. I still have this board today and it amazes me how many things I accomplished on it and how many things I still have to do. When creating a vision board please utilize my 33% strategy. One-third of your board should have photos and words highlighting previous achievements, one-third of your board should have photos and words highlighting your current and near future achievements and lastly, one-third of your board should have photos and words highlighting your lifelong desires. Again, the teacher in me would be remiss if I did not provide you with an example of my vision board. See Figure 4.2. If I begin to lose focus I am easily reminded of my goal simply by looking at any of my walls. My office is filled with my certificates, awards, and academic degrees. If you took a look at my screensaver and wallpaper on any of my electronic devices you will see I have The Noble Truth Project logo on it. Looking at this on my phone or iWatch automatically helps my mind acquire the Tunnel Vision which is necessary for me to execute my goal.

Figure 4.2

THE CLASSROOM THAT SMASHED THE TEST

When I first started teaching, I knew nothing about the trade. I learned from the very best educators in the State of Georgia, like Mrs. O'Connor. Mrs. O'Connor's room was amazing. Unlike other teachers whose walls were plain, her walls were filled with charts, posters, student work, affirmations, and mirrors covering her classroom walls. Everything on the walls was intentional and was used for instruction. I used to observe her first grade class during my planning period to watch her work. She would rarely use the whiteboard or traditional powerpoints. I hardly remember her opening up a textbook. She understood what her students saw was the most important thing. She had programmed the entire state curriculum within her student's subconscious mind. Her students knew Math and could read better than any first graders I'd ever met. When it was time for the state exam they smashed the test. They had the highest scores in both the school and the district. Mrs. O'Connor won Teacher of the Year for the second consecutive year. She taught me how important images were to learning. A lesson I have never forgotten.

The key to obtaining Tunnel Vision is to become aware of not only your visual but also auditory suggestions. WHAT YOU ARE WATCHING AND WHAT YOU ARE LISTENING TO MATTERS. My wife loves Beyoncé. I am not a big fan, however I know almost every lyric to her songs. I hear Beyoncé in the car, in the house, and at the gym. Because the songs became repetitive and I cannot turn off my ears, my brain slowly programmed the words into my subconscious mind. This is why I am unaware that I know all the words until the song begins to play. We must be intentional and ask ourselves, do these sensory suggestions help or hurt us in obtaining our goals? For instance, if ones' goal was to lose weight, I doubt watching The Food Network would be helpful; instead they should be watching fitness videos on YouTube. Instead of listening to the radio they may begin to tune into a specific podcast related to health and wellness. Your mind cannot focus on two things at once. THERE IS NO SUCH THING AS MULTITASKING. We must control our thoughts by utilizing the principle of Tunnel Vision. Turn off the television shows and musical selections that serve as a distraction and begin to tune into audio and visual content that will help shift your mind and turn your goal into a reality. As a personal development trainer, I studied the greats; Eric Thomas, Norman Vincent Peale, Napoleon Hill, Tony Robbins, Les Brown, Zig Ziglar, Bob Proctor, Paul Martinelli, Emile Coue, and John Maxwell. I watched and listened to almost every recording I could get my hands on. I read countless books authored by leaders in my industry. This is the only way one acquires Tunnel Vision, a necessary step in achieving success.

THE DRIVE TO WORK THAT MADE HIM MILLIONS

There once was a man who suffered a terrible car accident, totaling his vehicle. With lack of transportation, he and his wife began to share her car. He would wake up an extra hour early to take her to work and then drive himself to the office afterwards. On his way to work in his wife's car, the radio was programmed to her favorite playlist. One weekend went by where they both were driving out of town and the husband knew every word to his wife's favorite songs. He asked to change the playlist, but she refused claiming he must've liked the songs too since he knew the words. He knew all the words because of his drive to work. This 20-minute ride everyday programmed his mind with her playlist. After this weekend trip, the husband realized what had been done and he made a decision to effectively change his circumstances. He began to listen to a talk show that spoke about investments within the stock market. After several months of driving to work listening to his new station he successfully became a day trader. He knew exactly what stocks to buy and sell because of his daily drive to work. He ended up no longer driving to work as he began to work from home. He bought and sold stocks using just his cellphone. Those daily drives to work showed him the power of developing Tunnel Vision and enabled him to be one of the most profitable day traders I know.

My mentor, District Attorney Paul Howard, Jr. once said, "You can't be what you can't see." A powerful statement which I understood so intimately. In our weekly meetings, District Attorney Paul Howard would tell us to close our eyes and see a world free of crime. Many thought he was a little "crazy" but he understood the power of acquiring Tunnel Vision. The power of seeing your future success is critical. Experiencing your future is a vital component of Tunnel Vision and a vital aspect of The NOBLE TRUTH PROJECT philosophy. I remember when I used to have nightmares. I would wake up and swear the dream was real. I would wake up sweating and breathing. Dreaming or active visualization is a great strategy to influence the mind. As I woke up from my nightmares in a cold sweat, I realized the body responds to the mind and the mind cannot differentiate between a real experience or an imaginary experience.

While teaching yoga at several juvenile detention centers, the key to my students' success started in their own minds. I learned a skill set that I now call active visualization. Active visualization is the process of guiding a traditional meditation into a suggestive experience. Psychologist, Travis Bradberry and Jean Greaves explained a "MRI scans of people's brains taken while they are watching the sunset are virtually indistinguishable from scans taken when the same people visualize a sunset in their mind." This is a powerful NOBLE TRUTH. I would instruct the young men in my program to relax, breathe, and meditate while also speaking their future into existence. I would say things such as, "while you're breathing begin to imagine yourself walking across the stage to receive your high school diploma or GED, see your families' faces, hear the ovation as you walk across the stage to receive your diploma, feel the diploma in your hands." Experience does not have to happen in real life for the effects to be present within your mind, body, and spirit.

HOW TO VISUALIZE

The first step to meditation is to breathe. Meditative breathing requires you to be conscious of your inhaling and exhaling. It can be a variation of using both your mouth and/or nose. I tend to only use my nostrils but have also at times only use oral breathing. My guided meditations differ from several yoga instructors. I tend to guide my participants through awareness of their five physical senses. I strongly believe that in order to be fully engaged in a visualization one cannot be distracted by their five physical senses. When you quiet the five, the sixth sense will come to you, allowing you to utilize your five physical senses within your visualization.

1. Begin to notice your taste buds. Maybe your saliva and begin to not become distracted by your taste buds. If you become hungry or thirsty during your meditation do not act upon it. Let it go and return back to your breathing pattern.

2. Notice what you smell (maybe your perfume or cologne) and begin to not become distracted by whatever you smell. If you become aware of what you're smelling during your meditation, do not act upon it. Let the thought go and return back to your breathing pattern.

3. Observe what you are hearing. Maybe you hear the

noise in the next room and seek to not become distracted by what you hear. If the sound begins to slip into your mind during your meditation, do not act upon it. Let it go and return back to your breathing pattern.

4. The hardest step for me is when I begin to notice my movements. Maybe your hands and legs are not still. Begin to settle them and make a promise not to move during your meditation. Even if you have to scratch an itch, do not act upon it. Let it go and return back to your breathing pattern.

5. Lastly, begin to notice your sight, maybe you see other people or a photo in the background. Do not become distracted by what you see, simply close your eyes and return back to your breathing pattern.

6. By controlling your fives senses and breathing you are now meditating. Once you gain control over your meditation, begin to daydream, imagine, visualize you living out your dream. Envision yourself accomplishing your goal. Truly experience success by allowing your five physical senses to operate during your visualization.

This active visualization activity is critical to you developing Tunnel Vision. Putting your visualization into action is key to you obtaining success. Similar to an actor or actress, you must fully transform yourself into the person you wish to become. What we listen to and what we see everyday plays a major role in our thoughts, beliefs, actions, and results. IN ORDER TO INFLUENCE THE MIND GREATLY ONE HAS TO DEVELOP TUNNEL VISION. By using the strategies outlined in this chapter you can as Mahatma Gandhi stated, "be the change you wish to see." Becoming mindful about what your brain is exposed to is a vital part to your overall success. One must be intentional, in order to develop Tunnel Vision.

Tunnel Vision is a crucial step to acquiring success and cannot be overlooked. Do not move on without creating a vision board. Reading this book, watching my videos on YouTube, and listening to my podcast will help you develop Tunnel Vision. As you begin your personal development journey remember that there is power in listening to only one voice. Joining the NOBLE TRUTH PROJECT community for a considerable period of time will lead you one step closer to your desired goal. Remember the old saying, "an idle mind is the devil's play- ground." We cannot be bored as boredom will kill our dreams. We cannot afford to bounce around from program to program, book to book, podcast to podcast. Success starts and ends in the mind. Give the seed of this philosophy an opportunity to blossom within your life. There is always something we can be doing to achieve our goal even if it is playing a YouTube video or looking at your vision board. These small Tunnel Vision strategies will go along way in conjunction with the other five steps to success.

STEP FOUR: DEVELOP TUNNEL VISION SUMMARY GUIDE:

YOU MUST LISTEN TO MATERIAL ON GOAL
YOU MUST WATCH MATERIAL ON GOAL
YOU MUST READ MATERIAL ON GOAL
YOU MUST POST AFFIRMATIONS
YOU MUST CREATE A VISION BOARD
YOU MUST VISUALIZE YOUR DESIRED GOAL

5

GAIN SUPPORTERS: THE FIFTH STEP TO SUCCESS

 "Alone we can do so little; together we can do so much."

— HELEN KELLER

We all need the assistance of others to manifest our dreams. THERE IS NO SUCH THING AS SELF-MADE. It is not enough to solely obtain your goal we must be able to sustain it as well. The way to sustain any form of success is to attract the correct personnel to you. As a speaker and trainer, it is imperative that I partner with a great videographer. Videography is not my talent nor my passion, however it happens to be for my videographer. See, everyone has a role to play in the expansion of your dream. Leadership expert, John Maxwell affirms, "relationships are a major key to success." We all need supporters especially when seeking to sustain success. There are days in which I want to give up or take a day off. It is important that I have accountability partners to help me through these difficult days. Whether you have a personal goal or a professional goal, gaining supporters is an invaluable commodity. In order to properly attract the right people to you, you need to utilize the Gift of the Gab.

How do you gain supporters? The Gift of the Gab will enable you to attract the correct personnel to your team. The gift is knowing how to effectively utilize everyone on your team. Everyone is valuable, whether they offer their time, talent, or token. The gift is for you to master the art of finding out how every person can assist you. As a professional speaker I want to focus on just speaking, however to be successful I need to market my services and operate it as a business. I am not a videographer and I am not going to get my roommate to be my videographer either. I have the gift to understand not only what but WHO I need to attract into my life to "GROW MOORE." Self-help expert, Napoleon Hill called this the "Power of the Master Mind", defining it as the "coordination of knowledge and effort, in a spirit of harmony, between two or more people, for the attainment of a definite purpose." I needed others who were experts in their field that intersected with my field. After planning, I made a decision that I needed to hire a booking agent, accountant, graphic designer, and videographer. Their services are essential to me manifesting my dream of becoming a professional speaker. The Gift of the Gab starts with obtaining the gift. The gift is for you to master the art of finding out how every person can assist you.

THE SHOT

Athletic coaches are constantly planning and making deci-sions. One of the greatest coaches of all-time is basketball coach, Mike "Coach K" Krzyzewski. Since 1980, Coach K has served as the head men's basketball coach at Duke University, where he has led the Blue Devils to five NCAA Championships, 12 Final Fours, 12 ACC regular season titles, 15 ACC Tournament championships, and 5 gold medals including three consecutive Olympic medals. Coach K is the epitome of success as he leads the NCAA in all-time wins with over 1100 victories. In 1992, the NCAA Tournament was highlighted by a game between Duke and Kentucky in the East Regional Final to determine the final spot in the NCAA Final Four. With 2.1 seconds remaining in overtime, defending their status as national champions, Duke trailed 103–102. Coach K took a short timeout to use his GIFT. He met his team at half court and exclaimed they were going to "WIN." As a gifted leader, Coach K asked Grant Hill if he could make the 75 ft. inbound throw down the court. He also asked Christian Laettner if he could catch the ball. Little do people know Coach K planned for Laettner to take the shot if he was open but to also pass the ball to two other players. He made a decision to have Grant Hill throw a pass the length of the court to Christian Laettner, who faked right, dribbled once, turned, and hit a jumper as time expired for the 104–103 game win. Duke not only made the Final Four but won the National Championship becoming one of nine schools to win back-to-back national championships. This game was ranked #1 on the list of the greatest NCAA tournament games of All-Time compiled by USA Today in 2002 and in 2004 Sports Illustrated deemed it the greatest college basketball game of all time. The only reason Duke won their second straight national championship is because Coach K knew his personnel and has perfected the gift.

I have seen some great athletic coaches throughout the years, especially on the college level. The best coaches are the ones who can successfully recruit the best players. Best players not meaning all 5-Star recruits, but the best players for the overall team. A successful athletic coach must master the GIFT. They must be able to know how each player can be utilized to not only ensure victory but build camaraderie. Later on learn the story of how one coach in particular is such a master of the GIFT that he trusted a true freshman.

THE SAME ROLE AS HITLER

One of the most successful politicians is German chancellor, Angela Merkel. Like most politicians, Chancellor Merkel has developed a keen insight on how to gain supporters. Unlike her predecessor, Adolf Hitler, Angela Merkel has used her Gift of the Gab to help build a more peaceful nation. She firmly believes that all things are possible and can be with peace. When she first assumed office in 2005, Germany had a 12.6 percent unemployment rate, the highest since Hitler came to power in 1933. Most recently it dropped to under 5 percent – the lowest since reunification in 1990. Even though Merkel will be the second longest serving German Chancellor, she is the longest serving official to serve in the European Union. During her 2019 Commencement Speech at Harvard University, Merkel stated, "Change for the better is possible if we tackle it together. Going it alone, we will not succeed." She understands the power of operating as a team. Her humble beginnings as the daughter of a pastor and a teacher made her a passionate public servant. During her speech Merkel also encouraged the graduating class to "surprise yourselves with what is possible —let us surprise ourselves with what we can do". Her faith is unmatched living under the division of the Cold War. As the first female leader in Germany, winner of the Charlemagne Prize, and Presidential Medal of Freedom recipient, Angela Merkel has leveraged her supporters to gain tremendous results.

THE COACH WHO TRUSTED A FRESHMAN

I remember watching the University of Alabama's head football coach, Nick Saban on *60 Minutes* and it blew my mind! Nick Saban was called the "Perfectionist." The story opened up with his mantra, "Get Your Mind Right!" Nick Saban has amassed six national championships which includes five within the last 10 years. During this televised special, Coach Saban was seen at practice enthusiastically instructing players to "Do it again." He strives to not only make his players the best they can be, but also his coaches, staff, and even landscapers. In the documentary, Saban was seen fussing that the grass was not cut at the right length. He proclaimed that, "everyone must do their job." Coach Saban understands the importance of knowing his personnel. In the 2018 National Championship game, Alabama trailed Georgia 13-0 at halftime when Coach Saban made a bold decision. Gifted Coach Saban, removed his seasoned starting quarterback, Jalen Hurts and inserted a true freshman quarterback, Tua Tagovalia. In the fourth quarter, Tagovailoa led the Tide on a massive comeback and tied the game at 20-20 sending the game into overtime. In overtime, Georgia had a successful drive that resulted in a 51-yard field goal. On Alabama's first offensive play in overtime, Tagovailoa was sacked for a 16-yard loss, which seemed to be the end of the game, but this true freshman quarterback immediately followed up with a game-winning 41-yard touchdown pass. Freshman quarterback, Tagovailoa was named the Most Valuable Player of the game. The only reason Alabama won their 17th National Championship was because Coach Nick Saban knew his personnel and has perfected the gift.

Once you know what supporters you need, the next step is to attract them onto your team. Mastering the gab is the way I have been successful in recruiting others. The gab is an acronym meaning "Give, Ask, and Believe". Self-development specialist, Dale Carnegie asserts how to make people like you instantly is by obeying the law of human conduct, "always make the other person feel important." There's no better icebreaker than giving someone else something. THE ART OF GIVING IS A SIGN OF HUMILITY AND SACRIFICE WHICH IS CRUCIAL TO YOU GAINING SUPPORT- ERS. Giving can be associated with roses on a first date, giving a card during the holidays, or simply giving your employer a compliment after a business meeting. Next, your ask can make or break a relationship. Your ask will be more of an approach than an ask. Approach is my comprehensive term which identifies one's appearance, tone of voice, word choice, body language, and facial expression. All of these components matter when asking another person for assistance. Lastly, you must believe the relationship will result in success. When you truly believe, your give and ask will be genuine. This gab strategy has become even more prevalent due to social media. Social media expert, Gary Vaynerchuk proclaims, "you'll crush it as long as you concentrate on being yourself." Social media has made the GAB become quite lucrative. As people display their GAB, they will experience success. Just take a look at Cardi B, Tai Lopez, and Kim Kardashian. Every Instagrammer is banking on success based on how they gain supporters.

OKKURT

Anyone who can create their own word certainly has the Gift of the Gab. Cardi B became an internet celebrity after several of her posts and videos became viral on Vine and Insta- gram. She was seen telling stories of her experiences as an exotic dancer in New York City. Because of her charismatic approach to storytelling, she was awarded the opportunity to appear on TV. From 2015 to 2017, she appeared as a regular cast member on the VH1 reality television series, *Love & Hip Hop: New York*. She gave her audience something to talk about and in 2018, Cardi B released her debut album, *Invasion of Privacy*. Like most musical artists Cardi B, hit the road doing several interviews to promote and ask her fans for their support. Her fans responded as she has since earned three #1 singles on the Billboard Hot 100. Her hit song "Bodak Yellow" made her the second female rapper to top the chart with a solo album. *Invasion of Privacy* debuted at #1 on the Billboard 200, broke several streaming records, and was certified triple platinum by the RIAA. In her previous roles, Cardi B, always believed that she would be a successful rapper. Cardi B made her dreams come true as her debut album won a Grammy Award for Best Rap Album, making Cardi B the only woman to win the award as a solo artist. Among her numerous accolades, Cardi B has been awarded a modeling contract, several endorsement deals, and has even appeared in several mainstream movies. In 2018, *Time* magazine included her on their annual list of The 100 Most Influential People in the World. Cardi B, is a true example of how to utilize the Gift of the Gab to gain supporters and achieve major success.

Figure 5.1

THE CURRICULUM ON BROWN STREET

Morehouse College introduced me to the Gift of the Gab. The Gift of the Gab formula is the standard practice for those seeking to become a politician or pastor. I have been to several churches and campaign events led by my Morehouse peers and I have yet to be disappointed. All of these dynamic events featured them using the "Ole Morehouse Mystique, the GIFT of the GAB. I love preachers such as Creflo Dollar, TD Jakes, and Joel Osteen who have also mastered the GIFT of the GAB. Through their words they have inspired millions, directly changed the lives of thousands, and collectively made billions. The most successful preachers "Give, Ask, and Believe." Pastors start with giving, usually in the form of a song or a sermon, they then ask you to make a donation or tithe to the church, and lastly they believe you will join their congregation. Master salesman Zig Ziglar said, "if you will help others get what they want, they will help you get what you want." This format has created success for all who know how to use it, especially politicians. All politicians who wish to be successful should master the Gift of the Gab formula. I have seen it work in local, state, and national elections. Back in 2007, Barack Obama also became the master of the Gift of the Gab when campaigning for President of the United States of America. During all of his campaign speeches he focused on giving people hope. He asked his supporters for a campaign contribution, and lastly, he believed every single American would cast their vote in his favor. Because of the "GIFT of the GAB" formula, Barack Obama became the 44th President of the United States of America.

I remember in high school my friends and I would love to go to Jersey Gardens Mall. We barely had any cash to buy anything but we would go to "pick up girls." We would play a game and see who can get the most numbers before the movie we were seeing started and if we were really bold, we would see who could get a random young lady to attend the movies with us. These games taught me a lot about influence and gaining supporters. I realized whenever attracting a person of interest it is important to give them something first. YOU MUST GIVE IN

ORDER TO RECEIVE. You can give anything such as a card, a meal, or something as simple as a compliment. Who can turn down a compliment? No one. Everyone likes to be flattered. I would give my name and without prompting these young ladies would willingly tell me theirs. Psychologist Travis Bradberry and Jean Graves state, "greeting someone by name is one of the most basic and influential social awareness strategies you can adopt." I would say my high school, age, and where I lived, and most of the time the young ladies would automatically respond with theirs. I would not ask a question in which I did not answer first. Even though I no longer go to the mall for dates, I certainly use this model often when attracting new clients to my business.

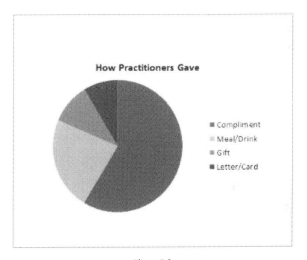

Figure 5.2

The Gift of the Gab is rooted in belief. Don't stop giving or asking. We must be persistent and always follow up. WE MUST BE OKAY WITH BEING VULNERABLE ENOUGH TO ASK FOR WHAT WE WANT. When I first had an idea to start The Noble Truth Project, a mentoring program I was met with quick denial. Probation officers, judges, and friends stated I was too young to start a nonprofit of such significance. They told me to continue to volunteer with their programs until I was ready. However, I was ready. I emailed the probation officers, judges, and court administrators everyday until I got a second meeting. During the meeting I laid it all on the line. I expressed my deepest sentiments to serve the youth. I even cried, tears poured down my eyes, because I wanted it so badly. Looking back on my proposal, I was certainly ill-prepared. The budget was off, the proposal had several typos, and the curriculum had several holes in it, but they accepted it because of my hard work and vulnerability. Motivational Speaker, Eric Thomas stated, "You have to realize you can't expect a full harvest when you are not willing to put your best effort forward." That opportunity changed my life and helped me to change the lives of others. The belief in myself ultimately gave me the confidence to launch this business and write the book you are currently reading. Do not be ashamed to believe, for you shall get whatever it is you desire. Remember, you receive not, because you have asked not. Seek and you shall find. Ask and you shall receive. Knock and it shall be opened unto you.

THE UNLIKELY CANDIDATE

There was once a young lady that interviewed for a supervisor position and was certainly unqualified, but still got the job. The job qualifications included having a master's degree, seven years of work experience, and proficiency in Excel. She possessed none of these qualities, amassing an associate's degree, two years of work experience, and never used Excel a day in her life, but she still got the job. She came into the interview with her hair, shoes, and wardrobe fit for the role of the Director. She answered the questions professionally and her facial expressions exuded confidence. We all knew she did not have the correct responses, but her body language and tone of voice indicated the opposite. We all saw her leadership skills from a mile away regardless of if she was "qualified" for the job. When we talked about her salary, she expressed her interest in earning more. She even stated that she would be unlikely to accept the position if the salary did not match her request. Two days later she signed an offer letter with her desired salary. I learned a valuable lesson. It is not always your experience or qualifications, it is your approach.

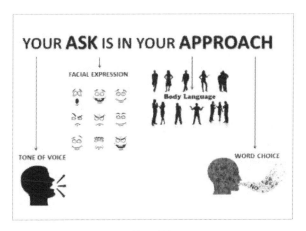

Figure 5.3

Working in the Fulton County District Attorney's Office introduced me to some tremendous lawyers, none greater than Mrs. Rucker. Her conviction rate was 100% as she never lost a trial. One day I knocked on her office door and I asked her how she became such a winning lawyer. She instructed me to sit down and asked if I was interested in becoming a lawyer. I responded, "No," but sought to have the same impact she had on the juror with my clients. She told me that being a lawyer is about the facts, but more so about conveying the story through your tone of voice, diction, and word choice. Depending on who her jury was her word choice would be reflective of that. She said she makes sure her diction is clear, especially if she had elderly people on the jury. Mrs. Rucker wanted to make sure the jury heard every word she said and lastly, her tone of voice changed depending on what evidence she presented in the courtroom. Law is simply persuading people to believe you. The facts are important but not as important as appealing to the people who will deliver the final verdict.

When you apply the Gift of the Gab principles to your interactions with others you will become successful. A team that you know and trust is key to you sustaining a positive effort to obtaining your goal. Look at President Obama or Oprah Winfrey, their successes are a result of gaining supporters. In John Maxwell's *The 5 Levels of Leadership* he states "winners attract people...the key to building a winning team is recognizing, selecting, and retaining the best people." The principles laid out in this book need to be practiced on a daily basis. Your ask should be animated and for that reason requires practice. Do not move onto the next chapter without practicing on your spouse, friend, or coworker. Practice in the shower or mirror at home. The art of persuasion is exactly that an ART. Gaining supporters through the Gift of the Gab can be mastered. Once you master the law of attraction, in collaboration with the other five steps you will obtain peace of mind, the ultimate success.

STEP FIVE: GAINING SUPPORTERS SUMMARY GUIDE:

COMMIT TO YOUR APPROACH
COMMIT TO YOUR APPEARANCE
COMMIT TO KNOWING YOUR PERSONNEL
COMMIT TO GIVING TO OTHERS
COMMIT TO ASKING OTHERS FOR HELP
COMMIT TO BEING HUMBLE

6

GET RESULTS: THE SIXTH STEP TO SUCCESS

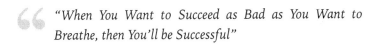

"When You Want to Succeed as Bad as You Want to Breathe, then You'll be Successful"

— DR. ERIC THOMAS

In order to succeed in obtaining your goal you must develop a healthy obsession. An obsession occurs by taking initiative, making decisions, creating plans, remaining patient, and having persistence. RESULTS COME TO THOSE WHO LOVE WHAT THEY DO. How do you get results? Every professional development program I've attended was centered around this theme, "Getting Results." Everyone wants to get results, however the tools lie within one's mind. World renowned Psychologist, Carol Dweck states the most successful people have a "growth-mindset," which she defines as a "belief that abilities can be cultivated." We must get results. No matter what your goal is, there are always positive results one can obtain during the journey. We must trust the process and adhere to the six steps during difficult moments and times of comfort. This NOBLE TRUTH is essential as it will boost one's self-esteem, confidence, and passion to continue on. The guiding principles to getting results are.

SHE FLIPPED AND GOT RICH

Having won a combined total of 30 Olympic and World Championship medals, Simone Biles is one of the most decorated gymnast of all time. She is an exemplary representation of getting results through a healthy obsession. Biles exhibited patience at a young age, she is the third of four siblings, all of who have lived in and out of foster care. Simone eventually lived with her grandfather and was introduced to gymnastics at age six. Coming from these unique and traumatizing circumstances, Biles has triumphed enabling her to have a tremendous amount of perseverance. By the age of eight Simone made a decision to be the best gymnast in the world. She set a definite goal and began immediately to actively train. Simone took the initiative and became obsessed. Working alongside her coach, Aimee Boorman, Biles and her family put a plan in motion to ensure her long term success. In 2012, Biles's grandparents switched her from public school to homeschooling, allowing her to increase her training from approximately 20 to 32 hours per week. This persistence boosted her gymnastics success and during the 2012 season led her to become one of the "Most Influential People in the World" by *Time* magazine.

Executing on a goal requires taking initiative. People take initiative based on making a decision. Making decisions are not easy but are necessary to getting results. DECISIONS DO NOT HAVE TO BE "RIGHT" THEY JUST HAVE TO BE MADE. When one makes a decision, it will inevitably be the "right" one. Indecision creates doubt and worry in the mind. When making a decision it should be based on your intuition and never your emotions. Be fully present while making a decision. Our emotions change, our intuition stays the same. Our minds love decisiveness and so do your clients and your employees. Once we make a decision, we must not change them. We must simply make another decision if the previous one was deemed unsuccessful. Decisions do not necessarily become easier, yet if we set a definite and SMART goal early on, our decisions will be easier to make in the future. Data is a component of making decisions but ultimately the best deci- sions will be made based on intuition. Decisions should also be based on alignment. My mentor Paul, once told me the 3D's of decision making. Either we 1) Do It, 2) Delegate It, or 3) Delete It. Decisions will only lead to more decisions. If you are able to make timely decisions, you will be able to obtain your goal and that's the NOBLE TRUTH.

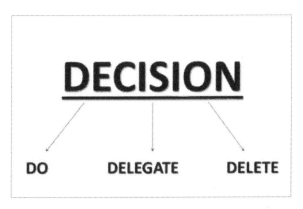

Figure 6.1

DECISIONS DECIDE DOLLARS

Decisions are difficult to make, but necessary for success. Joanna and Chip Gaines base their livelihood on making timely decisions. Joanna and Chip Gaines operate Magnolia Network, a home construction, home decor, and cooking business. With a net worth of nearly $20 million, they became a household name due to HGTV's hit show, *Fixer Upper*. The show walks you through the process by which the couple turns dilapidated homes with potential into showplaces that are helping to revitalize whole neighborhoods. I renovated my home in 2019, which required making tough, time sensitive decisions. On the show, Chip and Joanna would oftentimes take up an old floor and noticed it was not leveled. They would quickly convene with homeowners to make a decision. Do you want to 1) continue to lay the new floor, 2) repair the subfloors, 3) jack up the entire floor joist? Or with a leaky pipe do you 1) patch up the leak 2) replace the pipe, 3) replace your entire cast iron plumbing? Chip and Joanna made these types of decisions on a daily basis. When I began to renovate my home, I was making similar decisions and they were not easy nor were they cheap but I learned to trust my INTUITION and make the best possible decisions based on data, price, time, and expert opinions. At the end of the day, a decision has to be made in order to move forward. Nothing in our world stays still, everything is in constant motion. So if you are procrastinating you're not stuck, you are effectively moving backwards. All decisions are good ones as long as you continue to make them.

"You live and you learn" is a NOBLE TRUTH I live by. When things do not turn out as planned, I always learn a valuable lesson. Many people fall victim to procrastination because they are afraid of failure. If they begin to see their losses as lessons it would enable them to make a decision. YOU WILL NEVER GET THE RESULTS YOU DESIRE WITHOUT MAKING A DECISION AND TAKING INITIATIVE. Self-help guru, Napoleon Hill declares, "procrastination, the opposite of decision is a common enemy that practically everybody must conquer." I grew to make decisions based on my intuition and instinct as a young athlete. I have always been a natural competitor as I played sports throughout my childhood. At an early age, I learned that success comes as a result of hard work. Much of my time as an athlete was not spent in games but in practice. Practice is necessary in building one's intuition and instinct. We tend to think of practice as an athletic activity, however we can improve on any skill through practice.

CHESS CHAMP MAKES THE RIGHT MOVES

In middle school, I was deemed a chess champ, playing in multiple state and local tournaments. My dad taught me how to play at a young age and never took it easy on me. He taught me that in order to become successful at chess, I had to make quick decisions, I had to take the initiative. "The clock waits on no one," he said. He taught me the best way to make decisions is by planning ahead. A good player he said, "should have moves planned out five steps ahead." In middle school, I had my first ten moves mapped out. No matter where my opponent went, I would have my next move already designed. I knew where I wanted my opponent to focus and thus where they would move. I won so many games because I had made a decision. A skill I developed due to my planning, patience, and persistence. Due to my healthy obsession, I knew the moves they were going to make before they made them. It was magical to see what truly happens when we are fully present in the decision making process.

In order to successfully achieve your goal you need to not only take the initiative and make decisions but also plan. On a Sunday, my wife and I have developed a habit of planning for the upcoming week. Educator Stephen Convey explains, "habits are powerful factors in our lives. Because they are consistent, often unconscious patterns, they constantly, daily, express our character and produce our effectiveness...or ineffectiveness". We developed the habit of breaking Sunday down GET RESULTS: THE SIXTH STEP TO SUCCES into hour intervals. For instance, I iron all of my clothes for the entire week and she will begin to meal prep for the entire week. This type of planning requires a great deal of initiative and patience. Even though doing these habitual activities every Sunday can seem quite mundane they have been overwhelmingly effective. Make sure you organize your day. These essential character traits or habits are the key to us getting results.

Figure 6.2

THE ZEN MASTER

Phil Jackson has utilized planning and patience in becoming one of the greatest basketball coaches of all time. Phil Jackson was the head coach of the Chicago Bulls from 1989 to 1998, He coached the Bulls to six NBA championships. He also coached the Los Angeles Lakers from 1999 to 2004 and again from 2005 to 2011. The team won five NBA championships under his leadership. Jackson is known for his use of the triangle offense as well as a holistic approach to coaching that was influenced by Eastern philosophy. This approach to the game of basketball led to his nickname "Zen Master." Phil Jackson's philosophy of "one breathe, one mind" has produced great results. During the 2001 NBA Finals, Jackson had reserve Lakers guard, Tyronn Lue wear a sleeve during practice. The idea was to simulate for his players what it looked and felt like to defend against Philadelphia 76ers superstar guard, Allen Iverson, who always wore a sleeve during games. By emulating Iverson's sleeve, the Lakers entered the series with a slight psychological edge that helped them secure their victory. Every team he has coached has practiced mindfulness, meditation, and silent days evoking patience in all of his players. He developed a healthy obsession for his players. Phil Jackson's planning and patience awarded him 11 NBA titles as a coach, the most in the history of the NBA. He also holds the record for the most combined championships, winning a total of 13 as both a player and a coach.

In order to start The Noble Truth, LLC, I worked diligently planning things out. I have memo books on countless ideas and plans. I have had several plans that required me to exhibit patience. Sending emails and getting responses that informed me "to wait, hold on, or try again later." I remained persistent with my plans even though I had to practice patience. It was not long until my patience awarded me opportunities to APPLY my plans. The patience I endured strengthened my plans, so much so that my plans became habits of persistence. I executed tasks such as daily postings on social media, weekly meetings with my staff, and sending out quarterly newsletters to my email base. Getting results are a product of making decisions based on your plans, patience, and persistence.

FROM GED to PHD

Dr. Eric Thomas (ET) has been one of my idols since he burst onto the scene in 2013. His moniker "Succeed as Bad as you Want to Breathe" made him one of the greatest motivational speakers of all time. His motivation is derived from him being homeless, fatherless, and a high school dropout. In order for ET to become successful it requires not only patience but also persistence. As a teenager, ET fell madly in love with his now wife, Dede Mosley, who he followed to Oakwood College in Huntsville, Alabama. ET struggled in undergrad as he lacked the proper skills to excel in academia. Even though he had begun his career as a public speaker, he did not graduate college. He even created a successful GED program for under-served residents in the Huntsville area without obtaining his undergraduate degree. In 2001, ET finally received his bachelor's degree after completing 12 year of schooling. After years of struggling in school, ET mastered the art of patience and persistence and planned to enroll at Michigan State University to pursue a graduate degree. In 2005 he was awarded a master's degree in Education. After releasing his viral "Guru Story" on YouTube and publishing his own book there was no need to take his education any further. However, his pursuit of excellence led him to re-enroll in school for a doctoral degree. HE HAD MADE THE DECISION TO BE THE BEST. In spite of a busy schedule of traveling, speaking, and a family at home, persistence and patience afforded ET a doctoral degree in Educational Leadership and adorned him with the title of the "#1 Motivational Speaker in the World."

One thing I love about Eric Thomas is that he takes the initiative and promotes the "long game." He promotes the power of patience. Many people today don't exhibit patience. We want our food faster, our internet faster, and our success faster. Speed does not equate to success. When we rush, we tend to make mistakes. I grew up in the 1990's so I remember the beginning stages of the internet. I remember the old dial up connection when the AOL man was seen running across the screen. It would take minutes for one website page to load, now we are all upset as our devices slowly load four pages at the same time. My patience began to grow the more I learned about time. Time is Natural. Time is Nature. It is merely a reflection of the Earth rotating around the Sun. THE MORE WE ALIGN WITH NATURE, THE MORE OUR TIMING WILL BE RIGHT. Motivational Speaker, Eric Thomas said, "the secret to success is in the nature of the seed, not how long it takes to see results." Everyday, I take a moment to glance at the clouds, so I do not lose my understanding of time.

HOW A ROLLERCOASTER CHANGED MY LIFE

A major component to getting results is persistence. To be actively patient is to be persistent. I often speak to youth about the importance of active patience in which I use an analogy of Six Flags. Most youth at some point in their lives went to Six Flags or a similar theme park, where they waited in line to go on their favorite ride. I remember growing up, we visited Six Flags Great Adventure multiple times. My favorite ride was "Batman and Robin." When this ride first came out the lines were super long, averaging at least an hour. I remember waiting under the hot sun for the chance to experience the ride. Here's what I noticed about persistence and patience and why it is an important process in obtaining success. First, people would leave the line. Several people would get into the line and leave after a few minutes because they refused to wait. They wanted to get on the ride but they didn't have the patience to get on the ride, thus they would leave. This made my time in the line shorter. Another group of people attempted to cut the line saying, "Excuse me, my friend is up ahead," until they reached the front of the line. These individuals are sometimes successful but when they got caught they were either 1) kicked out the park or 2) sent all the way to the back of the line. Making their wait longer than mine. I realized the best thing for me to do was to practice active patience. Move when it's time to move, but remain disciplined by staying in the line. Similar to Aesop's

Fable "Tortoise and the Hare", as long as I was actively patient, I would get the results I desired and ride "Batman and Robin."

PERSISTENCE IS A DEFINING FACTOR IN ACHIEVING SUCCESS. Growing up I frequently saw hard-working individuals. None worked harder than the corner boys of Newark, New Jersey. Whether you go on Prince Street, Stratford Avenue, Isabella Avenue or any of the other well-known housing projects a corner boy would be present. A corner boy's work hours are well past a typical 9-5 and resemble more of sunup to sundown schedule. The neighbor– hood drug dealer on my block was Mo. Mo was always up and ready to make a sale. I would see him walking up the block before I headed to school in the wee hours of the morning and headed back down the block hours after I returned home. He would walk up and down the neighborhood making sales in the snow, rain, and during every holiday. Mo developed a healthy obsession, he took the initiative. He certainly had the heart of a hustler and taught me a valuable lesson in entrepreneurship. Take no days off. Business mogul, Grant Cadrone proclaims, "the very first step, and the most important one, is to commit all the way! This inescapable truth is that to be truly great at anything you must devote yourself completely."

People seem to criticize the person who is in a constant pursuit of greatness. They aim for mediocrity and would tell others to take a day off, relax, or take a vacation. Yes, these mental health days are essential to your growth but do not make them the norm. Success equals peace of mind. SUCCESS IS TO LOVE WHAT YOU DO AND BEING ABLE TO LIVE OFF OF IT. If you love what you do, you will never work a day in your life. Once you achieve your goal you can take as many vacations as you want. When I arrived at Morehouse College, I got a phone call that someone had shot Mo in the head. I prayed for his recovery and within two weeks, I received another phone call stating that he was back on the corner working again. If Mo did not work, he did not eat. He was committed! I certainly do not promote becoming a corner boy, but I am encouraging you to have the same work ethic as Mo. Mo had no true job, many felony convictions, and no high school diploma, but he has always been self-sufficient.

Your dream wants all of you not a portion of you. Every day, every hour, every minute is valuable in your pursuit of happiness. Benjamin Elijah Mays said it best in his poem, "God's Minute":

> "I've only just a minute, Only sixty seconds in it.
> Forced upon me, can't refuse it, Didn't seek it, didn't
> choose it, But it's up to me to use it.
> I must suffer if I lose it,
> Give an account if I abuse it,
> Just a tiny little minute,
> But eternity is in it."

We must be causative when achieving success. Taking action will win. DO NOT ALLOW YOUR PLANNING TO BECOME PROCRASTINATION. Every second counts. The best technique I learned to develop my patience, persistence, and planning came from my millionaire mentor.

THE MAN THAT WROTE

One of my mentors is an elder, millionaire who lives close by. My wife and I would visit his home which had high ceilings, it's own liquor room, and his own library. Every time we came over he would make us sign his guest book, putting the date and time we arrived. We called him the General as he served in the military and now ran his own financial consulting firm. On this particular day he led us up to his library as he wanted to show me one of his favorite books. While there, we glanced around and I saw several memo journals. I asked him what all the memo pads were for and he explained to me that those were his journals. Every evening he would write a page in his journal and had been doing this since he was 11 years old, he developed a healthy obsession. Now at 71 years of age, there were well over a hundred journals. He explained to me that he never wanted to make the same mistake twice, whether it was in business or a personal matter. So each day he would write about what he experienced and use the weekend to read through the previous week's journal. He stated, his business deals were a result of his journal entries. He had amassed a net worth of well over a million dollars due to his reflections. He improved on new and old projects by continuously writing them out in his journal. He had reached back out to old friends who became new clients. He never missed sending a family member or friend a card on their birthday. He had become a master planner by setting aside time every day to journal. He challenged my wife and I to do the same. Honestly, I have never been as committed as the General in this task, however I do now keep a journal and write in it as often as possible.

Writing down your thoughts are the first steps to getting results. Without action results will not occur. Results require you to be a decision maker and take initiative. Good decisions are based upon your planning, patience, and persistence but most importantly your intuition. Getting Results is a step that must be cultivated along with the other Steps to Success outlined in this book. Getting results is one of the most important things to do. Live by Napoleon Hill's words, "A quitter never wins and a winner never quits." It is an essential component to the NOBLE TRUTH PROJECT philosophy as well as the world. Successful people get results. In order to make your goal a successful one, we must be dedicated to planning, patience, making decisions, practicing persistence, and taking initiative. YOU NEED TO DEVELOP A HEALTHY OBSESSION IN ORDER TO BECOME SUCCESSFUL.

All of these qualities evoke action. Without results along the way, one's self-esteem and confidence will begin to fade and the support from others will be nonexistent. Be sure to promote your results no matter how big or small they are. SUCCESS STARTS AND ENDS IN THE MIND. I hang up all of my awards in my office, whether it is my degrees, certifications, or simply a certificate of appreciation. They all help me build my confidence in getting results. This step in unity with the other five steps identified in this book will garner you unlimited success.

STEP SIX: GETTING RESULTS SUMMARY GUIDE:

MASTER ORGANIZING EVERYTHING
MASTER REMAINING PATIENT
MASTER A HEALTHY OBSESSION
MASTER PLANNING FOR TOMORROW
MASTER MAKING DECISIONS
MASTER TAKING THE INITIATIVE DAILY

REFLECT AND REPEAT: OUTRO

This six step formula has been proven successful. Through careful application, I and numerous others have been successful in obtaining our goals. Throughout the years, I have returned to this philosophy over and over again. We must constantly GROW MOORE. Never stop pursuing your dream because what is a life worth living if you are not in pursuit of what you desire. SUCCESS STARTS AND ENDS IN THE MIND. Success equals peace of mind. Success is doing what you LOVE to do and being able to LIVE off of it. No matter how long it takes for your goal to manifest, you must keep going. Reflect and repeat these six steps. This Six Steps to Success formula has helped The Noble Truth Project turn gangsters into graduates, employees into entrepreneurs, and homeless individuals into homeowners. We seek to not only inspire you, but give you the implementation tools and strategies to achieve your desired goals.

If you are struggling, stuck, or failing to produce you need to set a definite goal. This key principle will teach you how to select the correct goal based on your desires and personal belief. Once you share your NOBLE TRUTH you will discover your

PROJECT. You must understand the power of setting a SMART goal. This essential step will lead you from a place of mystery into a place of purpose and success. Remember fear is a state of mind that you can overcome. FEAR IS MENTAL. In order to overcome fear you must be able to identify it. There are five mental fears that repeatedly hold one back from obtaining success. This second step will challenge you to look fear squarely in the face and discover your internal power to overcome them. Through sharing your NOBLE TRUTH you will acquire success.

To obtain any level of success, we must be mindful of our thoughts. We all experience negative thoughts that limit our beliefs, which ultimately drive our behavior. Our thoughts are reflected by what we say and how we say it. Success is a result of our thoughts, words, and actions. Learn what words to avoid and how to remove unwanted thoughts as you continue to further your education on how the human mind works. In the third step you have discovered the power of the subconscious mind. Procrastination is the enemy of all successes. SUCCESS REQUIRES INTENTIONAL FOCUS. Reread the specific strategies to help shift your mind and obtain tunnel vision. Through the use of imagination, autosuggestion, and repetition you will learn the ultimate principle of the NOBLE TRUTH PROJECT. This fourth principle will set forth a new world of unlimited ideas, freedom, and power.

In order for anyone to grow, you will need supporters. Applying the gab technique is a great way to attract the necessary personnel to help you move your goal forward. Continue to develop the skills to effectively create harmony amongst your team. Through this fifth step, you must effectively implement the gift of gab. Ultimately, to be successful you must yield results. Everyone wants results but not everyone knows the proper process to obtain results. Properly balance your persistence and your patience in order to get what you want.

This final principle focuses on the importance of organized planning, making decisions, and taking the initiative in order to achieve your desired goal. You need to develop a healthy obsession. SUCCESS COMES TO THOSE WHO ARE IN LOVE WITH THE PURSUIT OF THEIR GOALS.

My grandfather used to garden in his backyard. He would grow several crops, none more important to him than his tomatoes. I used to play basketball everyday in that backyard and he would just sit and watch me shoot. When I missed a shot the ball would ricochet off the rim and usually end up in his garden. He would shout, "Don't hit my tomatoes." I used to be so confused, because all I saw was dirt. One day, I walked up to him and said, "Papa, there are no tomatoes over there," and he told me, "The roots are growing." At that moment, I did not understand him. I walked away and continued to play, but reflecting on this profound statement it is the reason why we all need to show persistence.

"Your roots are growing," highlights that we will not see every victory along the way. The roots of a plant are underneath the soil, blind to one's eye but a sign that something is growing from the seed you planted. Your dream is akin to that seed. We must continue to water it, provide it with sunlight, and diligently protect it. The timing of the harvest is unknown. We will not see the roots of our dreams. However, the roots are the most important component of any plant. The roots allow the plant to receive water and nutrients to grow. The roots are what keep the plant stable in the case of storms or heavy winds. The roots are essential to the life of any plant. Be persistent with your goal, even if you do not see the fruits of your labor. Just know your roots are growing, a key component to your overall success.

Make sure you commit these six steps to memory as none is more important than the other. Only through the implementation of them all working in tandem will you reap the ultimate benefit. Reflect and repeat these six steps. Live your life to your highest potential by setting a goal, overcoming your fears, being mindful, developing tunnel vision, and gaining supporters, as you seek to get the results that you desire and that's the NOBLE TRUTH.

Ian Elmore-Moore is the Founder of the Noble Truth LLC, a mindfulness and leadership development company that specializes in professional and personal growth. Originally from Newark, New Jersey, Ian has been dedicated to shifting minds and changing lives.

At the age of 21, Ian co-founded The Noble Truth Project, a non-profit organization that ran a Saturday diversion program for adjudicated adolescents. Ian believes once you are able to share your NOBLE TRUTH you will discover your PROJECT. Through his leadership, the non-profit organization assisted hundreds of youth within the metro-Atlanta area, bolstering a 17% recidivism rate. This success led Ian to become Atlanta-Fulton County's Gang Prevention Coordinator, the first for the state of Georgia.

Ian has had several years of classroom experience as a certified middle school Social Studies teacher, where he became a two-time district nominee for Teacher of the Year. Ian is also a registered yoga teacher, who instructs trauma informed youth within Georgia's Department of Juvenile Justice facilities. Ian earned his Bachelor of Arts degree in Philosophy from Morehouse College and his Master's degree in Educational Leadership from Kennesaw State University.

Through meditation, observation, and personal experiences; Ian developed "GROW MOORE," a six-step success formula. Ian is a writer, professional speaker, and life coach, traveling around the world to assist students, educators, athletes, entrepreneurs, and business professionals in discovering their NOBLE TRUTH.

To work with Ian please contact us through any of the outlets noted above. We look forward to working with you to implement the six-steps to success formula. It's time to take the next step.

Made in the USA
Columbia, SC
22 April 2020